"Restaurant patrons looking for quality dining have Zagat to guide their cuisine needs. For the recruitment industry, the name is Weddle ... Peter Weddle that is."

American Staffing Association

Also by Peter Weddle

A Multitude of Hope: A Novel About Rediscovering the American Dream (due in 2012)

Job Nation: The 100 Best Employment Sites on the Web

The Career Activist Republic

Work Strong: Your Personal Career Fitness System

Recognizing Richard Rabbit: A Fable About Being True to Yourself

Career Fitness: How to Find, Win & Keep the Job You Want in the 1990's

WEDDLE's Guide to Employment Sites on the Internet (biannually, 1999-present)

WEDDLE's Guide to Association Web Sites

WEDDLE's Guide to Staffing Firms & Employment Agencies

Internet Resumes: Take the Net to Your Next Job

CliffsNotes: Finding a Job on the Web

CliffsNotes: Writing a Great Resume

WEDDLE's WIZNotes: Fast Facts on Job Boards (for different career fields and situations)

'Tis of Thee: A Son's Search for the Meaning of Patriotism

What People are Saying about WEDDLE's Books & Services

"A wealth of useful, updated information."

Library Journal

"This book is a great resource. … It's like a travel guide to job boards."

Corporate Recruiter

"Highly recommended!"

Richard Nelson Bolles, author of What Color is Your Parachute?

"When in doubt, consult WEDDLE's … an industry standard."

HRWIRE

"The WEDDLE's Guide to Employment Web Sites supplies clear, completely current information about each site's services, features and fees—helping users instantly determine which site best meets their needs."

ExecuNet, The Center for Executive Careers

"I found your book in the public library. Recently, I purchased my own copy from Amazon.com. It is a terrific book for breaking down the complexity of looking for a job. Thank you for writing this book."

Job Seeker

"…an incredibly useful tool in helping individuals focus their job search on the Web."

Career Counselor

The Success Matrix

Wisdom from the Web on How to Get Hired and Not Be Fired

Peter Weddle

ISBN: 978-1-928734-70-3

Special discounts on bulk quantities of WEDDLE's books are available for libraries, corporations, professional associations and other organizations. For details, please contact WEDDLE's at 203.964.1888.

Where People Matter Most

Contents

Introduction

I started writing a column about online recruitment for the interactive edition of *The Wall Street Journal* in the late 1990's. I wrote that column every two weeks for more than a dozen years, from the founding of Monster.com and CareerBuilder.com to the advent of social networking and the arrival of LinkedIn.com and Facebook.

During that same period, I also began writing a column about online job search and career success for CNN.com. That experience led me to write two books about the radically new dynamics of employment in America's post-recession, 21st century world of work. The books are entitled *Work Strong: Your Personal Career Fitness System* and *The Career Activist Republic*.

Today, I've transformed my two columns into online newsletters, one for recruiters and one for job seekers. The articles in *The Success Matrix* are a selection of those that appeared in the job seeker newsletter over the past two years. They present the insights I've gained and the strategies I've learned for achieving job search and career success, both today and into the future.

All of the articles have two distinguishing attributes:

- First, they are always frank and candid about the significant changes that have taken place in the American workplace. There's no sugarcoating the extraordinary effort that each and all of us must now exert in order to adjust to this new environment. Why? Because I think it's better to know the hard truth than the easier fantasy.

- Second, they are unabashedly optimistic. There is no handwringing over the significant challenges we face or over what we must do to overcome them. In fact, *The Success Matrix* is suffused with a single, defining theme: the American Dream is alive and well in the global economy, and the modern American workplace is filled with more opportunity than ever before. All we have to do is learn how to capture it.

So, what will you find in this book?

There are articles about what the post-recession job market looks like and how to leverage its dynamics to find a new or better job. And, there are articles about the post-recession workplace in the U.S. and how to harness its dynamics to hang onto and prosper in the job you already have. I hope you find all of them to be both inspiring and helpful.

Peter Weddle
Stamford, CT

Section I:
How to Get Hired
in a Tough Job
Market

What You Need to Know First: The Truth About the Post-Recession Job Market

Articles in This Section

NOTES

Why Employers Don't Hire Perfectly Qualified People

Today's turbulent economic environment has changed the way employers fill their vacant positions. Instead of using their traditional approach – hiring a person who is qualified for a job – they have turned to a new strategy that is best be described as "talent staffing." As a result, tens of millions of decent, dedicated and capable people – men and women who have successfully worked their entire lives – are now unemployed, unsuccessful in their search for a new job and unable to figure out why. No one has told them that the rules of the game have changed.

In the past, employers were willing to hire those who had acceptable skills and a track record of using them on-the-job. Today, they will only employ individuals who have superior skills <u>and</u> a track record of superior performance on-the-job.

In the past, employers were happy to hire qualified workers to fill their open positions and accepted that only a few would exceed their expectations, most would meet them, and the rest would need remediation and support. Today, they seek better-than-qualified persons – *people of talent* – and they expect them to contribute that talent to the organization's success from their first day of work.

What Makes Someone a Person of Talent?

In practice, employers have defined a person of talent to be someone who has one or both of two attributes:

- They have a skill that is critical to organizational success and a track record which demonstrates their ability to use that skill effectively on-the-job.

and/or

- They have a noncritical skill but perform at a superior level on-the-job which sets a standard that upgrades the contribution of everyone else in the organization.

Ironically, even though millions of Americans are now in the job market looking for work, a large percentage of employers believe there is a shortage of individuals with such talent. While their email boxes and mailrooms are filled to overflowing with resumes, they see themselves as increasingly challenged to find, recruit and retain workers who have the critical skills and/or the commitment to superior performance necessary for organizational success in the global marketplace. In essence, employers are convinced that only a very few people have talent and that talent is, therefore, in critically short supply.

While this view is their accepted wisdom, it is actually only half right. The truth is that every human being is born with talent – it is a universal attribute of our species – but sadly, only a very small percentage of people actually work with that gift. And because so few of us build our career on our talent, there is – for the moment, at least – a real and persistent shortage of that resource.

What Can You Do if You Are in Transition (or Worried That You Might Be Soon)?

First, make sure you know where your talent lies.

Talent is not singing and dancing and playing professional baseball. Talent is an inherent capability – an endowed capacity for excellence – which can be taught to do a certain kind of work. Talent may be a universal attribute, but it cannot be universally used. No talent is compatible with all work, but every talent can be expressed in more than one career field. It can be trained to perform in one occupation today and another tomorrow. But before you can do that, you have to know what your talent is.

Second, make sure you are working in a career field and for an employer that enable you to express and experience your talent.

Why is that so important? Because employers aren't hiring your profession, craft or trade, they're hiring what they think will be your performance. They want to hire all stars. Not people who are good at what they do, but people who are the best at that endeavor. And the only way you can be an all star – the only way you can excel at your work – is if you are working with your talent.

Yes, it's unfair that the rules of the game have changed. And yes, it's even more unfair that employers never bothered to tell anyone about it. But no, that change does not handicap you or put you at a permanent disadvantage. Quite the contrary, this shift to talent staffing is actually your Emancipation Proclamation. It frees you to find the work you love to do and do best and build a career with it. It liberates you to be a person of talent.

Come As You Aren't

For years now, we've had a "come as you are" job market. Basically, you looked for a new job with the skills you had in your old job. All you had to do, therefore, was update your resume, ship it out to a bunch of employers, do a little networking around the edges, and before long, you would have a couple of opportunities from which to choose. It was a simple, straight forward process, and unfortunately, it no longer works.

The "come as you are" job market was destroyed by trends which culminated in the Great Recession. Employers today no longer believe they can survive, let alone prosper, with workers who are simply qualified for their jobs. They need employees who are better than that – they want those who are accomplished in their field. And, despite all the people now looking for work, many employers believe there is a scarcity of such workers.

Where's the evidence? Consider this:

- According to a survey of employers by the National Association of Manufacturing, the Manufacturing Institute and Deloitte, one-third of all manufacturers say they can't find workers who can deliver the talent they need on-the-job.

- Almost half of all energy companies (43 percent) report similar shortages as do a whopping two-thirds (63 percent) of life science companies.

These are employers with open jobs they can't fill. Those vacancies exist, not because the employers can't find applicants – they have plenty of those – but because those "come as you are" applicants don't have what it takes to succeed in a cut-throat global marketplace.

Their shortcoming, however, are not permanent. Their situation is not hopeless … unless they want it to be. They can reinvent themselves; they can become accomplished individuals. And if they do, they'll have employers competing to hire them.

The "Come As You Aren't" Job Market

The world of work has now morphed into a "come as you aren't" job market. A lot of people don't want to hear that – they want to believe that things remain as they've always been – but that unfortunately isn't today's reality. The needs of employers have changed – not a little, but a lot – and either we adapt to their new requirements or we join the ranks of typewriters and rotary dial phones.

What does adaptation mean?

Instead of looking for a job as we were, we must now look for a job as we need to be. To achieve success in this new job market, we must always be changing, always growing, always getting better at what we do. We cannot allow ourselves to grow stale or to stand still, but instead, have to strive constantly to become accomplished. We must, in short, be forever recasting ourselves into what we aren't … yet.

What does such a person look like? How can you recast yourself as an accomplished individual?

From an employer's perspective, of course, such candidates have a number of attributes, but the three most important are:

State-of-the-art expertise in their field.

The only way employers can succeed in today's highly competitive marketplace is if every worker performs at their peak.

What could prevent you from convincing an employer you can do that? If you aren't currently enrolled in or haven't successfully completed a training or educational program in your occupation in the last 12 months, you are likely to be viewed as obsolete … no matter how many years of experience you have.

Ancillary skills that give them flexibility.

The global workplace is in a state of constant flux, so employers need workers who can effectively switch into and out of a range of different venues and situations.

What could prevent you from convincing an employer you can do that? If you aren't able to prove that you speak a second language, effectively use advanced technology on-the-job and/or work collaboratively in alternative settings (e.g., on teams and task forces, by telecommuting and in virtual organizations), you are likely to be viewed as rigid and limited … no matter how willing to change you may be.

A commitment to contributing on-the-job.

The margin between success and failure is so small these days that employers can only afford to hire those who deliver a meaningful impact on-the-job and do so from day one.

What could prevent you from convincing an employer you can do that? If your resume shows only what you can do and not how well you do it, if it indicates that you showed up for work but doesn't prove that you accomplished anything, you are likely to be viewed as a risky hire … no matter how perfect you think you are for the job.

The "come as you aren't" job market can sound like a very unforgiving place. And in some respects, that's true. There is no tolerance for those who want to do just enough to get by. It has no place for those who are content to be mediocre at their work.

However, for those who keep their expertise up-to-date and deliver it with impact wherever it's needed on-the-job, this new environment can set their fortunes to soaring. It empowers them to transform themselves from an ordinary job applicant to an extraordinary person of talent and to be seen as such by employers. It encourages them to become someone who isn't stuck with who they are, but is, instead, determined to reach for the best of who they aren't … yet. And, that's a ticket to unbounded success in today's world of work.

The Other Cause of Long Term Unemployment

A lot of us have been unemployed for a very long time. The conventional explanation for this situation is that layoffs have forced more workers to compete for fewer positions. While that's true, it is not the only reason – nor even the most important one – that so many people remain out of work for so long.

The other and primary cause of long term unemployment is a change in employers' expectations. They are no longer content to hire qualified workers. That's the reason so many job seekers get no response, no interview, no call back – nada – even when their application clearly indicates they meet one hundred percent of an opening's stated requirements. Employers may say that's what they're looking for in a new hire, but in reality, they expect more.

Employers today are battered by turbulence. They face new and escalating competition in both their local and overseas markets. They must satisfy an increasingly cost-conscious consumer who is also becoming more fickle about products and services. And, they are continuously pressured to keep up with the unceasing introduction of new technology and better practices.

To compete in such an unsettled environment, employers need workers who have two traits:

• they must be expert in their profession, craft or trade;

and

- they must be committed to maintaining that expertise.

The first trait defines a qualified person. The second indicates they are also a "career activist."

A career activist is a person who recognizes the fleeting nature of their ability to contribute on-the-job and therefore takes proactive steps to ensure their qualifications are always at the state-of-the-art.

Why is that important? Because a qualified person can do a job today, but may and probably will not be able to do so tomorrow. In the unsettled environment of the global economy, every job is constantly in flux, and only a career activist has the capacity to adapt.

How do you become a career activist and, no less important, how do you prove to employers that you have? The following will get you started.

Transforming Yourself

Becoming a career activist begins with acceptance. You must acknowledge that the "come as you are" workplace of the 20th Century no longer exists. The turbulence of the 21st Century economy means that nothing is settled any more. In effect, you must get comfortable with the one thing we humans hate most: change. You must be willing to expect it, plan for it and put it to work for you.

Then, you have to back up that acceptance with action. In the 20th Century, you could get away with paying attention to your career once a year – during your annual performance appraisal and salary review. In today's workplace, you have to work on increasing the strength, endurance and reach of your career every single day. In short, you now go to work to do your job <u>and</u> to do all of the things that will ensure you can continue to do so.

Proving Your Activism to Employers

Once you've adopted that kind self-improvement philosophy and made it an integral part of your workday, you will start to develop a record that employers will appreciate. It will demonstrate your ongoing acquisition of skills and knowledge in both your primary field and in ancillary areas that will enable you to use that expertise in a broader range of workplace situations. It will also reflect your ever greater visibility and stature among a continuously expanding network of professional contacts. And, it will underscore your commitment to working on challenging assignments with top flight organizations and high performing peers.

Those are all the hallmarks of a career activist's record. It is comprehensive in scope and, ironically, it will make you look incomplete. It will portray you as a person who is never satisfied with where you are, but always seeking to be more of what you can be.

If you're in a job search, for example, it will detail the learning you did in each of your jobs. After you describe the tasks you performed and the accomplishments you achieved, it will include a statement that begins with the phrase "What I learned" and concludes with a list of the knowledge you acquired. That entry is an employer's proof positive that you are, in fact, a career activist.

The long term unemployment that so many people are enduring today has its roots in structural changes occurring in the global economy. Its manifestation in the workplace is a significant and permanent shift in what employers expect in their new hires. Unlike in the past, they are no longer content with qualified workers. They want (and need) to employ qualified workers who are also career activists.

Three Job Market Fictions

It's hard enough to look for a job in today's tight economy. Doing it with a fictionalized view of the job market can dramatically degrade your chances of success. What are such fictions? They are pipe dreams and urban legends, to be sure, but increasingly, they are also misinterpretations of conventional wisdom. They begin with the right idea, but come to the wrong conclusion. Here are three of the most harmful.

Fiction #1: A job search is an interruption in your career.

The conventional wisdom is that a job search creates a gap in your record. And, gaps drain your perceived value as a new hire. Rightly or wrongly, recruiters believe that a gap is evidence that you're out-of-date in your field and out-of touch with the latest challenges at work.

Gaps come in all sizes, of course, but the larger the gap, the more explaining you have to do to employers. Why have you been unable to land a job? What's kept you from being hired by other employers? Is there something that's not on your resume that we should know about?

Gaps signal a break in your career progression, and employers seek candidates who have a steady record of progress in their work. It's a misinterpretation, however, to think that job searches create gaps. They don't. In fact, gaps exist only if we permit them to. A break in your growth as a high value performer occurs only with your permission.

How can you avoid a gap? The minute you find yourself in an active job search, enroll in a training program or academic course that will sharpen your skills and add to your perceived value as a candidate.

Then, feature that development on your resume. Show employers that you're determined to remain a high value contributor even while you look for a new employment opportunity. You'll both impress them with your initiative and eliminate the doubt a gap in your record creates.

Fiction #2: The best place to find a job is on a social networking site.

The conventional wisdom is that social networking sites are now the single best way to find a new or better job. According to pundits, LinkedIn, Facebook and Twitter have eclipsed if not replaced job boards, traditional face-to-face networking, print publications and career fairs as viable job search resources.

While such hyperbole gets media attention, it is a misinterpretation to think that these sites are all you need to find a job. Social networking is indeed a valuable job search tactic, but it is not the sole technique for conducting a job search or even the most effective. Indeed, for every person who has successfully found a job on a social media site, there are literally hundreds of others who have found employment using other tools.

In my 2010 Source of Employment survey, for example, we had almost 1900 people tell us that the single best way to find a job was by using a job board. Answering a job posting or archiving a resume on such a site was selected by over 28 percent of the respondents. The second highest response was a tip from a friend at 9.6 percent, followed by a newspaper ad at 8.4 percent, a call from a headhunter at 7.1 percent and a referral by an employee of the company at 6.4 percent.

Does that mean you should ignore social media sites? Absolutely not. But, take the chatter about the power of these sites with a grain of salt and use all of the tools at your disposal. Today's job market is the toughest in years, and you simply don't know which resource will end up working best for you. The key to success, therefore, is to play the odds and use every single one of them.

Fiction #3: There are no jobs to be found in the job market.

The conventional wisdom is that the stuttering U.S. economy is simply not creating new jobs. For example, according to the U.S. Department of Labor, there was a net loss of 93,000 jobs in September of 2010. This hemorrhaging of employment opportunities has produced an entirely new kind of job market. If we had a "jobless recovery" after the 2001 recession, we are now enduring a "less jobs recovery." Employers are simultaneously seeing their revenue and profits rise and shedding jobs from their structure.

While a lot of job seekers have been disillusioned by this situation, it is a misinterpretation to think that the job market is bereft of opportunity. In fact, the private sector actually created 64,000 jobs in that same month of September, 2010. And, there are other openings being created by voluntary separation. That's right, people are actually quitting in this economy to look for something better. The U.S. Bureau of Labor Statistics reports that more people resigned (2 million) between February and April of 2010 than were laid off (1.7 million).

Does that mean it's now easy to find employment? Of course not. But, it would be a tragic mistake to give up because you don't think there are any openings available. The jobs are out there, but it does take more than simply sending in a application to land one.

The key to success is not to shotgun an application out to every job you could conceivably perform, but instead, to focus on the smaller number of positions where you perfectly fit the stated requirements and can prove you will excel at your work. Then, do everything you can to stand out.

Network online and off to find a person in the organization you know who would be willing to refer you to the recruiter with the opening. And, look for professional blogs and other discussion forums online where employees of the organization tend to hang out and add substantively to their conversation. In short, make it your job to convince employers they can't succeed without you.

The conventional wisdom can clearly be helpful when you're looking for a new or better job, but make sure that you draw the right conclusions. Misinterpretations of even the best insights or most accurate data create fictions that can undermine and even derail your ultimate success.

Make Yourself Indispensable

A college economist recently opined that we have entered the era of "the disposable worker." Employers can and will toss out workers whenever they no longer need them or can find someone better. What he didn't say, however, was just as important. We have also entered the era of "indispensable talent" and that gives all of us the power to find and hang onto the job of our dreams.

To make sense of the new importance of talent, we have to first understand what it is. Contrary to popular mythology, talent is not a select skill or extraordinary accomplishment. It is not reserved for Lady Gaga and the winner of the Super Bowl. Talent is the capacity for excellence and an attribute of our species. Everyone has been endowed with the gift of talent. We all can excel.

Why is excellence now indispensable to employers? Because global competition has meant that they are no longer competing with cheap labor. They are going toe-to-toe with other companies that are employing well educated, highly motivated workers performing at the top of their game. As a consequence, American companies cannot survive let alone prosper with workers who do just enough to get by or are content to languish in mediocrity.

Now, before you rise up in righteous indignation, I am NOT saying that unemployed people are obsolete or substandard performers. What I am saying is that everyone – those of us in transition and those of us who currently have a job – are going to have to work smarter and harder than we ever have before. Not because we've been deficient, but because our competitors are more proficient than they've ever been.

The good news is that every single one of us is a "person of talent." We all have the inherent capacity to excel. To reach that level of performance, however, we will have to take two important steps.

Resetting Yourself for the New Job Market

Whether you're 22 or 62 or anywhere in between, the formula for finding a great job or hanging onto one is exactly the same. You have to be working at your talent and at the top of your game.

What does that mean?

Your talent is the intersection of passion and practicality. It is what you love to do and do well. If you're making a ton of money but have to drag yourself out of bed to go to work each day, you're not working at your talent. If you've built a career in a field where you're competent but unchallenged, where you earn a decent living but no sense of satisfaction, you're not working at your talent.

Why is that important? Because when you're not working at your talent, you cannot perform at your peak. You may be doing O.K. today, you may even be maxing out on your performance reviews right now, but the day will come when even your best won't be good enough. Why? Because you'll be competing with people who are working at their talent, and they'll have what it takes to excel.

So, **Step 1** is to do a little self exploration. Turn off the cell phone, tune out of iTunes and get to know yourself better. If you are working at your talent, great; proceed to Step 2. If you aren't, however, take the time to figure out just what is your capacity for excellence. You deserve to know. And, to have it at the center of the one-third of your life you'll spend at work.

Once you know your talent, you then have to determine which occupations will enable you to work with it. I realize that's easier said than done, but there are both private and public resources that can help. Among the former are professional career counselors and coaches while among the latter is the U.S. Department of Labor's free O*Net database, located online at www.onetonline.org.

In today's highly competitive economy, however, working at your talent is only half the answer. Unfortunately, it's possible to be in the right field and still not perform at your peak. How? By disrespecting your gift. By not providing your talent with the skills and knowledge you need to put your talent to work.

So, **Step 2** is to care for your talent. In today's economy, the value of your occupational expertise is directly tied to the pace of technological innovation. According to Moore's Law, the power of technology doubles every two years. As a result, the half-life of your skills and knowledge is now down to just twelve months, regardless of your profession, craft or trade. In essence, you have to be continuously reinforcing your ability to excel – even when you're working full time or looking for a job.

Today's unforgiving economy confronts each and all of us with a choice. Will we let ourselves be designated a "disposable worker" or will we reset ourselves as an "indispensable talent?" Will we continue to do things as we always have or will we tap our innate capacity for excellence and beat our global competitors at their own game?

Today's Two-Times-Two Job Markets

We've always known that there is more than one job market. For years, we've been counseled that there is the visible job market of job postings and classified ads and a "hidden job market" where openings are usually filled by referrals and networking. Those two markets continue to operate, but each is itself now divided into a labor and a talent market. They represent two very different ways of looking at working men and women and, therefore, provide job search experiences and employment opportunities that are equally dissimilar.

Whether it's visible or hidden, the labor market is one in which people are viewed as interchangeable cogs in a commercial system. In economic terms, job seekers are a good that can be acquired in the very same way an organization purchases the chairs in which its employees sit. Indeed, in some companies today, recruitment has been moved out of the HR department and into the purchasing department where it can be administered like a well oiled machine.

How can we tell if that kind of market exists in an organization? All we need to do is look at its corporate career site on the Internet. A labor market is present if:

- visitors to the site are treated as generic candidates – if, for example, sales and IT candidates are given exactly the same information about what it's like to work for the organization;

and/or

- the site has the look and feel of a store – if every interaction seems to lead the visitor to a transaction, to setting up a deal between a buyer (the employer) and a seller of labor (the candidate).

There may be some of us who prefer that kind of relationship with an organization, but most of us, I suspect, would rather be treated more respectfully. We are not widgets, but working people who deserve to be acknowledged as individual persons of talent.

The Talent Market Alternative

A talent market is one in which employers seek to find and hire individuals who are better than qualified for their openings. That doesn't mean they're overqualified, but rather that they are "ultra-qualified." They meet all of the requirements for an opening <u>and</u> are able to prove that they both can and will excel at their work. Employers believe that these persons of talent are rare so they will often compete to find them and pay recruitment bonuses and above market compensation to hire them.

How can we determine those organizations that operate a talent market? Once again, the corporate career site will provide the insight we need. A talent market exists if:

- visitors to the site are treated as intelligent and valued consumers – if they are given in-depth information about what it's like to work in the organization and that information is tailored to reflect the unique interests and concerns of those in their occupational field;

and

- the site has the look and feel of a farm – if every interaction seems designed to nurture familiarity and trust, the two pillars of a healthy relationship, between the employer and the individual.

Are there other ways to tell what kind of job market exists in an organization besides what happens at its career site? Absolutely. But that site is an easy evaluation tool to use, and with today's two-times-two job markets, it's essential that we make such assessments before making a move. Why? Because a labor market might help us get a job, but only a talent market will connect us with the challenging and rewarding work we deserve.

How Recruiters Work and Why

Recruiters. From a job seeker's perspective, they are a strange tribe. But maybe they aren't as weird as they might at first seem. Maybe there are good and important reasons why they do what they do. This article is the first of a three-part series that will explore *what recruiters want from job seekers.* If you're in transition or think you ever will be, make sure you read all three.

For many job seekers, recruiters are an odd breed lacking most or all of the traits job seekers associate with their own peers in the workplace. Recruiters seem to have a very different set of priorities and often to act in ways that simply don't make sense to those who operate in line units. The first step in understanding what recruiters want from job seekers, therefore, is to gain an accurate picture of how recruiters work and why. Let's do that by examining the complaints that job seekers typically voice about recruiters.

> *Job seekers, often complain about how long it takes for a recruiter to select even the first round of qualified candidates for an opening let alone the one person who will actually be offered the job.*

It is true that an open position can remain that way for weeks, sometimes months and even occasionally a year or more. For job seekers, the situation can be exasperating and even demoralizing. But, there are at least three reasons why such delays happen.

First, recruiting is an overhead function in virtually every organization and one deemed especially expendable during an economic downturn when there isn't a lot of hiring going on. During the last recession, in particular, many organizations significantly downsized their recruiting teams. Often, those layoffs have meant that fewer staff are now doing more work which means that all of a recruiter's openings get filled more slowly.

Moreover, the load isn't light. A recruiter can be responsible for filling 15-20 requisitions at a time. And for each of those openings, they have to work with the hiring manager to develop a position description, then figure out where best to advertise and source for the opening, then post those ads and perform those sourcing activities and finally, pre-screen all of the applicants just to get to the first round of qualified candidates.

Second, hiring managers – not recruiters – typically make the decision about who will be hired. Unfortunately, however, hiring managers are not evaluated on how well they staff their organization, but on the results they achieve with their unit. So, hiring managers often see the work involved in evaluating, interviewing and selecting a new hire as a lower priority than the mission of their unit, even when a vacancy will clearly make it harder for them to accomplish that mission.

In addition, hiring managers do, from time-to-time, change their minds. They decide to specify a different set of requirements for an opening or to look for a different kind of person to fill the job and those adjustments inevitably stretch out the recruiting process.

And third, because of the continuing high levels of unemployment, any opening that's advertised on a job board or in a print publication is likely to generate dozens, sometimes hundreds and occasionally even thousands of applications. While virtually every other function in the corporate headquarters can rely on technology to manage such massive inflows of information, the recruiting team cannot.

There are no artificial intelligence programs capable of screening those applicants. The recruiter must do so him or herself, and they have to do it in a way that ensures qualified applicants aren't overlooked and unqualified applicants aren't approved for further screening and interviews.

*Job seekers often complain that recruiters don't seem to have any
knowledge of their field or a good understanding of what's involved
in doing a certain kind of job.*

This complaint is often correct, but there's also a reason for that. The
first to go in the layoffs noted above are typically the most expensive
employees, and that includes the experienced recruiters who have spent
the last five or ten or more years actually recruiting for engineers or
nurses or salespeople. Then, when business picks back, many organizations don't rehire those experienced recruiters, but instead, try to save
money by bringing on new or relatively inexperienced recruiters who
must learn on-the-job.

Whether they are experienced or not, however, in most cases, recruiters are not themselves the kind of people they are trying to recruit.
They are recruiting professionals, not engineers, nurses or salespeople,
even though they are responsible for filling such positions. There are,
of course, exceptions to that rule, and experienced recruiters do acquire significant knowledge of the field for which they recruit. The fact
remains, however, that in many cases, recruiters know less and sometimes far less about what it takes to do a job than anyone who would be
hired to do it.

*Finally, job seekers also complain about the lack of flexibility
among recruiters and their unwillingness to consider anyone who
isn't an exact match for their opening.*

This complaint is also often true, and there's a reason for that, as well.
You see, recruiters are typically evaluated on how well they serve their
customers. Those customers are the hiring managers who have openings in their units. In fact, in many organizations, hiring managers actually fill out a customer satisfaction survey each time a recruiter works
on one of their openings.

While there are clearly exceptions, many hiring managers are not
especially articulate when it comes to describing what kind of person they are looking to hire for an opening. They often don't devote
much time to developing a detailed position description so the recruiter has to follow up and try to pin down the specific requirements

for a candidate and then determine which of those requirements are essential and which are nice to have. In effect, the recruiter tries to create a template against which they can then measure the qualifications of various candidates.

Because the recruiter is not expert in the field for which they are recruiting, they lack the understanding that would enable them to deviate from those stated requirements. They do not have the background or expertise to say, "Well the candidate doesn't have this specified skill, but they do have another one which compensates for what they are missing so let's keep them under consideration." In effect, recruiters look for people who best match the hiring manager's explicit requirements – that template they created – not because they are inflexible, but because they believe that's how they best please their customer, the hiring manager.

There's no denying that recruiters often seem to take illogical steps or engage in inefficient behavior during the recruiting process. Just as often, however, there are good reasons for the way they work. The key to success, therefore, is not to fight or get frustrated by their practices and procedures, but rather to accommodate and, if possible, leverage them to your own benefit.

How to Stand Out With Recruiters

This article is the second in a three-part series focusing on *what recruiters want from job seekers*. The first article explored how recruiters work and why. This article will address an equally important topic: how to be a standout candidate with recruiters. There are many ways to do so, but I believe there are five key steps you should take. I call them the **Five Phenom Factors** – the five steps that will set you apart for all the right reasons.

Phenom Factor #1

As I explained in the first column of this series, recruiters are very pressed for time. They can be juggling 15-20 openings at any one point, and the only way they can possibly get all of their work done is to have very efficient procedures. It does no good to install such procedures, however, unless every single candidate adheres to them. So, one way to stand out with a recruiter is to prove that you can follow directions.

For example, if a recruiter specifies that they want candidates to embed their resume in an email message when applying for a job, don't attach it. If they specify that you should attach your resume, don't embed it. Follow directions.

Similarly, if a recruiter schedules an interview for 9:00 AM, don't show up at 9:15 or 9:30. If they ask you to send in additional information right away, don't send it in two days later. Follow directions.

Phenom Factor #2

The second thing recruiters want from job seekers is a sense that they are really interested in the opening for which they are applying. They want to know that candidates have read and carefully considered the recruitment ad to which they are replying. They don't have the time to waste on throw-away applicants – those who apply for virtually any job that sounds interesting to them whether or not they are qualified or even interested in the work. So, another way to stand out with recruiters is to prove that you care.

When applying for a job, don't describe your qualifications with a generic resume that could be sent in for just about any opening. Show that you care about the opportunity by investing the time and effort to tailor your resume so it describes how your specific credentials match the specific requirements the recruiter has stated for the opening.

What recruiters don't want, however, is a candidate who cares too much and pesters them with daily emails about the status of their application. Granted, not every recruiter shows job seekers the simple courtesy of keeping them informed about what's going on, but one of the fastest ways to irritate recruiters is to stand out by being a pest.

Phenom Factor #3

The third thing recruiters want from candidates is the truth. They hate being misled by inaccurate or false claims, whether they're made on a resume or in an interview. They know that, unfortunately, a fairly large percentage of people exaggerate or misstate their credentials so a third way to stand out with recruiters is to reassure them they are getting straight information.

Recruiters are going to be double-checking everything you submit and say so learn how to provide persuasive responses. There are, of course, boundaries to what recruiters can ask you – they cannot question you about your religion or marital status or sexual orientation, for example – but as long as they are within those boundaries, you should always be honest and straightforward when answering a recruiter's questions.

If a particular matter or incident doesn't put you in the best light, it's not only appropriate, it's essential that you provide a full explanation of your side of the situation. There are, however, three rules that you should follow when doing so:

- One, admit mistakes if you've made them. Recruiters often like to see that candidates have the self-awareness to appreciate when they've slipped up and that they have learned from the experience.

- Two, rehearse what you're going to say about a less than flattering situation so that you don't sound defensive or cocky or, worst of all, indifferent. Recruiters like candidates who have the self-confidence to speak calmly and rationally about difficult issues.

- And three, never badmouth a former employer or boss, even if you feel you've been unfairly treated. Recruiters want to know that you won't be speaking ill of their organization should you be hired and then subsequently leave for another employer.

Phenom Factor #4

The fourth thing recruiters want from job seekers is preparation. Candidates who apply on a lark are seldom able to participate in the recruiting process efficiently or effectively. As a result, they slow the process down and, worse, increase the odds that it will be derailed for some unexpected reason. So, a fourth way to stand out with recruiters is to enter their process ready to be evaluated and raring to go if selected.

How can you demonstrate that you're prepared?

- First, recruiters want you to think through and rehearse the best way to present your qualifications for their opening. They don't want to have to wait while you struggle to figure out how to articulate what you've done or how that background is relevant to the job they are filling. You don't have to be a public speaker, but you do have to be able to describe clearly why you think you should be hired for the position.

- Second, recruiters want you to have done your homework on their organization and thus be able to ask good questions about it. What are good questions? They are those that provide you with the information you need to (a) understand the mission, values and culture of the organization and (b) make an informed judgment about whether you would like to work there. What you should ask about, therefore, is not the obvious stuff you can find on your own – like what kind of benefits the organization offers its workers – but rather information only an employee can provide – like how work actually gets done in the organization.

Phenom Factor #5

The fifth thing recruiters want from job seekers is good manners. The "finalists" they select will be presented to hiring managers to interview and consider for their openings. Given that those hiring managers are their customers and that the managers' satisfaction is a big part of their own performance evaluation, recruiters cannot afford to be embarrassed by a candidate who acts unprofessionally during those interactions. A fifth way to stand out with recruiters, therefore, is to give them the confidence that you will represent them well to their peers.

How can you convince them you will?

- First, dress the part. As part of the homework I mentioned in Phenom Factor 4, make sure you find out what kind of dress is the norm for the organization. If it's business formal, don't arrive in slacks and a polo shirt. If it's business casual, don't walk in dressed in a suit. Follow the lead of the organization.

- Second, be polite. Or to put it another way, remember what you learned in preschool. Treat others as you would like to be treated. So, begin each request with a please and end every interaction with a thank you. That includes the interview, should you have one. Always thank both the recruiter and the hiring manager for their time and interest in you and, if you want your message to stand out, send it by old fashioned postal mail rather than by email. Email is acceptable, of course, but text messages aren't.

So, let's summarize: recruiters may often seem to take illogical steps or engage in inefficient behavior during the recruiting process, but there are good reasons for the way they work. The key to success, therefore, is not to fight or get frustrated by their practices and procedures, but rather to accommodate and, if possible, leverage them to your own benefit. In short, you want to know and take advantage of the Five Phenom Factors. They'll ensure that you stand out with recruiters for all the right reasons.

How the World of Work Has Changed

This article is the third in a three-part series focusing on *what recruiters want from job seekers*. The first article explored how recruiters work and why, while the second discussed how to stand out with recruiters (for all the right reasons).

This article will address a topic that's every bit as important as the first two. It will discuss how the world of work has changed in the last five years so you understand what's causing recruiters to act differently in today's job market and why you have to adjust, as well.

As I explain in my book, *The Career Activist Republic*, the Great Recession changed everything in the world of work. It put a punctuation mark on trends that had been developing for at least a decade and, in the process, it forged an entirely new kind of workplace in the United States of America.

This new norm in the world of work affects everyone in the workforce. Male and female. Young and old. Its impact is as great on those who have just graduated from college and are looking for their first job as it is on those who've got years of experience under their belt and are looking for a new or better opportunity.

While there are a number of facets to this new environment, the single most important one for working men and women is this: *the tenure of employment positions is now dramatically shorter than it has ever been before.*

Most of us know that the days of working for the gold watch – of being employed for an entire career in a single organization – have been gone for quite some time. What many of us haven't recognized, however, is that the jobs we do have are going to last for such a short period of time.

For example, according to Spencer Stuart, an executive search firm, the average tenure of a Fortune 500 CEO is now down to less than four years. In other words, when a CEO takes on his or her new job, they can expect to be in that position for four years or less. And, if that's true at the top of the heap, you can be sure it's the same at every other level in the organization.

What's driving this significantly shorter job duration? In a word: uncertainty. It is the fact that employers can no longer count on what they thought they knew about the global marketplace.

Technology is advancing so rapidly, competitive pressures are rising so dramatically, consumer tastes have grown so fickle, and destabilizing events around the world – from wars and revolutions to earthquakes and reactor meltdowns – are occurring so frequently that no employer can predict what will happen six months from now, let alone a year or more down the road. To put it bluntly, the global economy that produces our jobs has become totally unpredictable.

So, What Are Employers Doing?

How are employers dealing with this totally new and unsettled environment?

Well, obviously, some have stuck their heads in the sand and are pretending it isn't happening. Most, however, are developing their own version of a common sense strategy. They are engaging in what might best be described as "rapid adaptation."

These employers know they can no longer achieve success by standing still – by doing what they've always done – so they are adjusting as rapidly as they can to the changes going on around them. And, those adaptations are changing the nature of the work they need done and thus the jobs and kinds of employees they require to implement their plans. In essence, they are doing away with the organizational chart and now operating with an organizational compass. And, every time they shift direction, they change their staffing requirements.

What does that mean for those of us in the world of work? Permanent employment will now be much less permanent.

A person once wrote that what most Americans want is "an honest to goodness, full time permanent job," and that's probably still true. What has changed is that the definition of such a position now looks uncomfortably like "an honest to goodness full time here-today-gone-tomorrow job."

We used to tell people that they would likely go through seven or eight job changes during a thirty year career. Well, that's now old news. In today's world of work – in the 21st Century – people are likely to go through fifteen or twenty job changes during a fifty year career. To put it another way, they are now likely to be changing jobs every three years or so.

Some of those changes will be to new roles within their current employer and some will be to entirely new employers, but in every case they will be dealing with a recruiter.

You see job openings are actually filled from two populations: those employees who are already working for an organization and those job seekers who want to. In fact, according to one survey, just over half of all new openings in large employers are now filled by internal mobility, by a current employee moving from one assignment to another within the organization. Even though the process involved in making that happen is dramatically less complicated than the traditional recruiting process, it is still under the control of the recruiter. They still determine who gets through the door and into the realm of consideration for all of the openings that will be filled from within.

The rest of the openings will be filled by external or new hires and there, of course, the recruiter is in charge, as well. They may not control who gets hired, but they definitely determine who gets considered. In most recruiting processes, it is the recruiter who conducts the initial pre-screening of all applicants and thus who is invited in for an interview with the hiring manager. In addition, it is the recruiter who oversees any background and reference checking that is conducted and can, therefore, influence how the findings of that research are presented. Think of it this way: a recruiter may not be able to select you for the job you want, but they can definitely ensure that you don't get selected.

So, the reason for learning what recruiters want is very simple. From now on, you are going to be interacting with them far more often than you ever have before in your career. In many if not all cases, the quality of those interactions will determine the quality of the jobs for which you are considered and ultimately hired. Recruiters don't have to become your new best friend, but you must understand how they work and why and how you can be a stand our candidate with them. That's the single best way to ensure success in your career.

The American Dream

While it is a quintessentially American aspiration, each of us has a unique vision of just what is the American Dream. For some, the dream is a chance to build a successful business. For others, it's a home of their own. And for still others, it's the opportunity to shop until they drop. As alluring as all of those visions are, however, I would respectfully suggest that they are outcomes of the dream and not the dream, itself. You see, the American Dream is actually a state of mind.

We all know, of course, that the American Dream exists because we live in a nation founded on certain extraordinary principles. Much as we take them for granted, deep down inside, every American knows that they are especially fortunate to live in a land where they are accorded an enduring right to Life, Liberty and the pursuit of Happiness. While most of us are very clear about what Life and Liberty mean, however, there is some confusion about the pursuit of Happiness. And it's that misunderstanding which causes us to misperceive the American Dream.

The founding fathers, themselves, inadvertently provoked this situation with their capitalization choices. They used initial caps on Life, Liberty and Happiness, when what they really meant to enshrine was a commitment to Life, Liberty and the Pursuit of happiness. In other words, what the American Dream promises is not a right to happiness, but a right to Achieve it on our own.

What Does That Mean for Those of Us in the Workforce?

Over the past decade or so, social scientists have been trying to figure out just what happiness is and where it comes from. While many of us think the answers to such questions are intuitively obvious, it turns out that we may be selling ourselves short. Humans have the capacity not only to experience happiness, but to experience joy, as well. And those two states are very different.

Joy is an emotional state. It is derived from our relationships with family and friends. When those interactions engage and satisfy us, when they enable us to be the best of ourselves with the others in our Life, we experience joy—one of the human species' greatest gifts.

Happiness, on the other hand, is a cognitive state. It occurs when we are tested by meaningful challenges that stimulate us to express and experience our fullest natural potential – our talent. These challenges can occur anywhere, but they are most prevalent in the workplace. In other words, our best shot at Achieving happiness occurs when we put ourselves in a position to excel at what we love to do.

That is the essence of the American Dream. It is a personal commitment, a determination to devote our Life and exercise our Liberty to the accomplishment of two tasks:

- To discovering our natural talent or what we love to do and do best;

and

- To working only where we can use that talent to achieve satisfying goals.

The outcome of those tasks will be unique to each of us, but the tasks themselves are the same for all of us. They represent our right to the Pursuit of happiness.

Those same two tasks are also the key to a successful job search and a rewarding career. Whether we're in transition or currently employed, they enable and empower us to control our destiny, to shape it to an end that is important and fulfilling to us. It is our right, to be sure, but it is also our responsibility. For only we can take the first step, only we can decide to set off on our own personal Pursuit of happiness.

Why should we bother? Because as wonderful as the joy is in our relationships, we deserve more. We spend at least one-third of our lives at work, and that experience should offer more than frustration, anxiety and despair. It should be – it can be – a source of profound fulfillment. Or what the founding fathers called Happiness.

What You Need to Know Next: Job Search Tactics That Actually Work in the New Job Market

Articles in This Section

The Job Market Version of Catch 22

Isn't Free a Four Letter Word?

How to Deal With What Used to be Called Failure

Job Retraining is Worthless

You're Only Kidding Yourself

The New Rules of the Game

Tiger Job Seekers

The 50-50 Job Search

The Application Two-Step

The Secret to an Effective Resume

The One Word You Should Never Use

A "Perfect" Stranger

The Dilemma of a Wimpy Job Seeker

The Two Best Ways to Find a Job All-in-One

What General Petraeus Can Teach Job Seekers

NOTES

The Job Market Version of Catch 22

Billions of words have been written about job search tools and tactics in this job market of our discontent. Job board dos and don'ts. Twitter. Facebook. Building a personal brand. Improving your "findability." It's all good advice, but none of it will work if your career is sick. To put it in another and admittedly blunter way, don't bother looking for a job if you have a wimpy career.

You see, that's what's different about today's job market. "Come as you are" has been replaced by "come as you aren't … yet." The good old days of searching for employment with stand pat qualifications are gone. If you're out of work, your career needs resuscitation.

It doesn't matter that you got superior ratings on performance appraisals in your last job. It makes no difference that you have a track record of being loyal, dependable, and hard working. And, it is totally irrelevant that your employer (a) went out of business, (b) was acquired or (c) was ineptly led and that (a), (b) or (c) was the cause of your unemployment.

The plain, hard truth is that employers view people in transition as damaged goods. It's not fair. It's certainly not true. And it stinks. But it is reality. You won't find many recruiters who will admit it. And in most cases, they work hard to avoid the appearance of such a bias. But deep down inside, it's there. An everyday event confirms it: when presented with a choice between two equally qualified candidates, one employed and the other not, the offer will almost always go to the person who already has a job. It's the job market version of Catch 22.

So, what can you do?

Reinvent yourself. It doesn't matter how well educated, trained or senior you are in your field, change your image in the job market.

How? By fixing your career. By building up its strength – its fitness. There are many techniques involved in doing that, but perhaps the most important is pumping up its cardiovascular health. The heart of your career is your professional expertise, so go back to school. Right now. Even as you are looking for a job.

Build Career Fitness

Revitalizing your career in the middle of a job search involves two important steps:

- **Step 1:** Begin acquiring a new skill or refreshing one you already have. You might, for example, take a course in a second language at a local community college or attend a new certification program offered by your professional or trade association. You can choose almost any topic just as long as it will clearly and meaningfully enhance your ability to contribute on-the-job.

and

- **Step 2:** Add the fact that you're back in school to your resume. Note it in the Summary at the beginning of that document and, describe it in its Education section. Provide the name of the course you're taking, the institution or organization that's offering it, the formal outcome if there will be one (e.g., the certificate or degree you will earn) and the term "Ongoing."

Those two simple steps will instantaneously transform you into a new person. First, they will enhance your skill set, making you a potentially more valuable employee. Second, taking a course of instruction or training program even as you are searching for a job demonstrates attributes all employers want but find it hard to identify in a candidate: resolve, fortitude, and determination.

Most importantly, this course of action will set you apart from other candidates by demonstrating that you have two very special attributes: you understand that in today's rapidly evolving world of work, staying competent in your field is an ever-moving target AND you take personal responsibility for keeping yourself at the state-of-the-art. You recognize the responsibility and accept it.

Become that person, make that transformation, and the playing field will level. You may be in transition, but you will no longer be at a disadvantage when compared to employed candidates. You will have reinvented yourself as a career activist, a person who is committed to continuous self-improvement no matter how senior or experienced they may be. An individual who has the right stuff—the skills and the attributes to be a champion at work.

Isn't Free a Four Letter Word?

Four letter words are generally thought to be unfit for public consumption. We counsel our kids to refrain from using them, and we do our best to abide by our own wisdom. It's odd, therefore, that so many of us seem determined to rely on a four letter word when we search for a job and manage our careers. What is this seemingly inoffensive term? It's the word "free."

Well meaning institutions and counselors often avoid programs and tools that require job seekers to pay a fee for their use. They argue that the cost imposes an inappropriate burden on those who are in transition and potentially experiencing financial hardship. They also contend that many if not all of the fee-based services can be obtained for free – there's that four letter word – on the Internet.

Certainly, no one can argue with the notion of trying, wherever possible, to avoid asking job seekers to sacrifice any more than they already are. To say that every product and service they might need should be free, however, takes that view to an illogical conclusion. Why? Because their good intentions have at least two unintended consequences that are bad.

Sending the Wrong Signal

First, advising job seekers (and others) that they shouldn't pay a fee for a product or service that can help them find a job or advance their career is the equivalent of saying they shouldn't invest in their future. We pay for our college education, our insurance policies, even our membership in a professional or trade association because we believe that doing so will benefit us, and we know it's up to us to do it. The same is true with our careers. There is no entitlement to workplace success, so it's up to us to make it happen. If we ignore that responsibility, we undermine our future.

Sometimes, the tools we need will be free – searching the employment opportunities on a job board, for example – and at other times, there will be a cost to acquire them. Paying that fee is not inappropriate; it's a commitment we make to and in ourselves. We have to be smart about it, of course – as with other kinds of investment, it is possible to buy useless or even harmful career products and services – but the payment itself is a profoundly empowering act, one that reinforces our self-respect and our capability at the same time.

Ignoring Qualitative Differences

The Internet is the richest source of human knowledge ever devised. It's also a garbage heap of mediocre advice, bad information, stale ideas, and occasionally, outright dangerous opinions. Most of us have learned, therefore, to evaluate what we find online very carefully. We select what we determine to be true and useful and we ignore the rest.

Subscriptions to the online version of The Wall Street Journal, for example, have actually risen during the recession, and those subscriptions aren't free. Hundreds of thousands of people pay to access that information because they believe that it's helpful to them and better than what they can get in other places.

The same is true with job search and career resources. There's a lot of free stuff out there on the Web, but it's not necessarily state-of-the-art or very helpful. For example, you'll find countless primers and checklists of job search techniques that worked in the 1990's, but will waste your time and get you nowhere today. Paying a fee for a career tool or resource doesn't necessarily mean it will be qualitatively better, but it certainly holds it to a higher standard.

So, what should you do? Be as smart a consumer of career tools as you are of cell phones and television sets. Assess the credibility and track record of the individual or organization behind the product or service before you invest your time or money in using it.

Now, I grant you that "free" is not your run of the mill four letter word. It's neither impolite nor off-putting. It is, however, potentially misleading and even harmful, at least when it's used to guide the way people acquire job search and career management resources.

What's a better way to judge such tools? Focus on how helpful they will be to you. You deserve access to the tools that will serve you best, and having to pay a fair price for them isn't doing you a disservice; it is making a down payment on your hopes and dreams.

How to Deal With What Used to Be Called Failure

Most of us go into a job search thinking we may be a little rusty, but confident that, basically, we know what to do. Then you get into it, and the galling indifference and humiliating rejection begin. Employers don't acknowledge your resume submissions; executive search and staffing firms don't return your calls; and recruiters act as if you are damaged goods. It's hard not to feel as if you're a failure.

And yet, you're not. Let me say that again: you are not a failure. You are not a loser or a deadbeat or a flop. Your belief that you are (or your concern that you may be) is based on two misconceptions. First, you think your career should unfold in a straight line. And second, you believe that today's job market is just like those of the past, only tougher.

Those views are widely held, and they are completely wrong. They may have been correct in the 20th Century, but today, they're as accurate as a stock broker's predictions. When you buy into them, therefore, you throw yourself into a well of defeat that leaves you believing that you've done something wrong. Or, that you haven't done something right. Whichever it is, the conclusion you draw is the same: you've let yourself and your family down.

It's a terrible self-indictment, and you don't deserve it. Let me say that again: You are not a failure. Only you can get rid of that feeling, however, and there's only one way to do so. You have to clear up those misperceptions. You have to view the job market and the workplace as they actually are. Not as they used to be or you wish they were. Do that – see today's world of work for what it really is – and you will turn what used to be called failure into what is now genuine success.

Correcting the Misperception of a Straight Line Career

You have probably never thought about it much, but if you're like most of us in the workforce, you assume that a career will unfold today just as it did in the last century. Your progress in the workplace will trace a straight line. You'll begin at point A and if you do well, you will move up to point B and from there, you will advance to point C and so on. Ever onward and ever upward.

The image of this traditional kind of movement, of course, was the "career ladder." It prescribed one way up and you either kept moving along the rungs or you fell off, got pushed off or retired. The dynamic was Darwinian, but at least you always knew where you stood.

Well, that career ladder is now gone. It's been tossed out by employers that can no longer support the human resource management infrastructure to manage your career for you (and everyone else). The straight line approach has, as a result, been replaced by the zigzag career. Ever forward, but not necessarily always up.

The image of this new kind of movement is the "career jungle gym." As you may recall from your schoolyard days, the jungle gym had two alluring qualities.

- First, you got to pick your own way forward – there was no teacher and, today, there is no employer telling you where to go.

- And second, sometimes you might move straight up, but occasionally you would move from side-to-side and even down and around to get where you wanted to go.

There was no discredit, disgrace or dishonor in the path you picked, because (a) everyone got to pick their own way and (b) if you kept your eye on your goal, you would eventually get there. The same is true with your career.

Correcting the Misperception of a Normal Job Market

It would be reassuring, I guess, to believe that today's job market is just like the ones of yore, only tougher. If that were true, we would at least know the rules of the game. Unfortunately, however, it's not. The rules have changed, and we must adapt if we want to succeed.

Historically, we had a "come as you are" job market. In other words, the skill set you had in your last job was sufficient to find a new job. All you had to do, therefore, was update your resume, send it out to a bunch of employers, do a little networking around the edges and bitta-bang, bitta-boom, you would land a job that was as good as or better than the one you had before.

Today, the opposite is true. If you are in transition, the skills you had to be effective in your last job are not sufficient to secure a new one. If you have any doubt about that, consider this: recent surveys have found that more and more employers are stipulating that unemployed persons should not apply for their openings. Why? Because, whether it's true or not, they believe the employed person is more capable and therefore more likely to make a valuable contribution to their organization.

How can you overcome such a disadvantage? You have to reinvent yourself even as you are looking for a job.

- Update your skill set or add a new skill that will enable you to apply what you can already do in a broader set of circumstances.

- Promote your new expertise by offering to speak at a meeting of your professional association or authoring an article for its member publication or Web-site.

That kind of initiative demonstrates that (a) you understand the importance of always getting better in today's workplace and (b) you take personal responsibility for doing so. Those two attributes will help to set you apart in the job market and restart your career.

Looking for a job in the current environment is definitely frustrating and often discouraging. It does not, however, make you a failure. Let me say that again. You are not a failure. What's happening today is simply proof positive that the rules of the game have changed. If you change with them – if you correct the way you look at the job market – you'll have what it takes to turn what used to be called failure into the modern definition of success.

Job Retraining Is Worthless

Job retraining is a waste of time. That's the conclusion of study conducted by the U.S. Labor Department (DOL). After studying the experience of 160,000 laid-off workers who went through DOL subsidized training programs, it found that the education neither helped them land a job nor hang onto one if they were able to get hired.

Does that mean you shouldn't bother with additional education and training if you're in transition? Absolutely not. But, there's a right way and a wrong way to go about upgrading your skills. And, the key to success is to recognize the difference and immerse yourself in the kind of retraining that will actually help you.

Job retaining is just that. It trains you to pursue a certain kind of job. There's nothing wrong with that … if you've done your homework.

For example, a recent article in *The New York Times* recounted the experience of an administrative assistant who was laid off in early 2009. The state unemployment office urged him to upgrade his skills so he spent six weeks in a training program on word processing and spread sheets. He finished the course, updated his resume and hit the bricks. And, he's still out there looking for work.

Why? Because, as the Department of Labor's own research shows, the job market for administrative assistants is shrinking, not growing. If this person had been given that research or done his own simple browser search for it on the Web, he would have discovered that the retraining he was being urged to take was preparing him for a career that was disappearing

What's a better alternative?

Ditch job retraining and take "career retraining" instead. That's not semantics; it's an entirely different way of viewing education for employment.

What Is Career Retraining?

Unlike job retraining, which focuses on acquiring the skills for a certain kind of job, career retraining prepares you for a career – multiple jobs – in a field of work. It involves several tasks before you even step into a classroom.

First, find an occupational field in which you would enjoy working and have the innate talent to succeed.

I realize that being in transition exerts severe financial and other penalties, so you want that time to be as short as possible. Nevertheless, investing the effort to acquire true self-awareness before you start off on your search will dramatically increase both your short and your long term prospects of success.

Second, figure out which way the winds are blowing in the workplace.

Nobody's crystal ball is perfect, but there is plenty of information about which fields are growing and which are being overtaken by technological innovation, consumer preferences and other change agents in the economy. Acquire that insight, and then, pick an occupation in which you would enjoy working, have the innate talent to succeed and are likely to be employed for awhile. Said another way, chase a dream you can count on for at least the next 5-10 years.

Third, become an expert in two fields: the occupation you selected for your near-to-midterm employment and the management of your own career.

In the 20th Century, up-to-date skills usually provided career success.

In the 21st Century, they are necessary but insufficient. Today, you need state-of-the-art skills and an equal capability in career self-management.

Being an adept manager of your own career enables you to evaluate the counsel you receive from others and to acquire the information you need to make informed choices on your own. You'll know how to steer around the obstacles that affect everyone in the modern workplace and what to do (and when and where to do it) to keep your career moving forward.

It would be nice if one could say that a single six week course adding a few skills is all it takes to get reemployed in this lousy economy. But, that would be untruthful. It would be great to claim that finding a job in today's world of work is just like finding a job in the last century. But, that would be unrealistic. The 21st Century workplace has been completely recast, and it's that new environment for which we should be retraining.

You're Only Kidding Yourself

I've been unemployed in my career. Twice. So what I'm about to say is based as much on personal experience as it is on a lifetime of studying the best practices for successful career self-management. There's a single, profound truth in hunting for a job: you're only kidding yourself if you think it will be quick and easy. It won't.

Whether the economy is in recession or firing on all cylinders, whether you're starting out in your career or have years of experience under your belt, whether you're a skilled tradesperson or a senior executive, looking for a decent employment opportunity is the hardest job you will ever have. It will take every bit of knowledge you can muster, every insight you can gain, every piece of wisdom you can acquire, and even then, it will take pluck, determination and plenty of hard work.

That's why I was absolutely stunned to see the results of a poll reported recently in *The Economist*. They found that unemployed workers in the U.K., Sweden and Germany devote 10 minutes or less per day to looking for a job. That's people who are unemployed mind you. They either believe they are entitled to a job—wishful thinking in today's global economy—or that pixie dust will make it happen for them—the employment equivalent of buying a lottery ticket.

Job search efforts were better in Spain and France, but nowhere near what's required for success. Unemployed workers in those countries spent 20 to 30 minutes per day searching for a new job. And in the U.S., the survey found that unemployed workers spent barely 40 minutes per day looking for a new employment opportunity. That's less time than average American spends watching television (4.7 hours) or getting showered and dressed each day (53 minutes).

What's the big deal?

Most of us will spend one-third or more of our lives at work. Doesn't it make sense, therefore, to invest the time necessary to get it right? Isn't it worth the effort to acquire a knowledge of the key principles and skills of effective job searching and then to practice them rigorously until you land a good job – one that will enable you to excel? Aren't you more likely to see a real and sustainable return on such an investment in yourself and your future than you are in an investment with (allegedly) smart stock market analysts?

Why, then, do so many of us sell ourselves and our careers short? Why are we spending so little time on the one wealth creation activity we can actually profit from and control?

A Matter of Misunderstanding

I can't say what's behind the less than vigorous efforts of workers in other countries, but in the U.S., I think it comes from a misunderstanding of the Declaration of Independence. That wonderful document, of course, defines our culture. It establishes our expectations both in our neighborhood and in the workplace. And subconsciously, many of us believe that the Declaration of Independence guarantees us Life, Liberty and Happiness. It doesn't. It entitles us to our Life, our Liberty and our pursuit of Happiness.

The word "pursuit" may be a noun, but it describes a state of action. It is the act of striving for something – in this case: Happiness. In other words, the Declaration of Independence accords us the opportunity to strive for a fulfilling and rewarding job – and despite its all too obvious faults, the U.S. delivers on that promise better than any other country on the face of the earth – but it's up to us to do so. We have to take the steps that will achieve our goal. We have to turn the potential for personal success and happiness into reality. Only we can create our own version of the American Dream.

Yes, there will always be exceptions to that rule. There will always be the lucky handful among our peers who have a great job drop in their lap. But for most of us, finding that job – a job that will engage and fulfill us – requires that we invest a meaningful level of time and effort. What's meaningful? Think of it as an equivalency. The Happiness you derive from a job search is equal to the personal commitment you make to execute it. So, give yourself a full 8 hours of Happiness each day on-the-job by spending a full 8 hours of searching each day for the job that will enable you to do so.

The New Rules of the Game

Finding a new job is a very serious game these days, and it's been made all the more difficult by a change in the rules. Historically, employers hired qualified candidates to fill their openings. Now, they don't. The key to success, therefore, is to understand what employers are looking for and to position yourself in the job market as just that kind of person.

For decades, working men and women have counted on a simple rule of thumb in the job market. If you matched the advertised requirements and responsibilities for a job, you were qualified, and if you were qualified, you would definitely be interviewed and maybe even hired. The rule made sense and it worked, so a lot of people came to count on it.

Over the years, however, "qualified" evolved into "good enough." If a person was good enough to do a job, they were good enough to be hired. That approach produced a "normal" distribution of capabilities in the workforce. Employers discovered that only a few of those good enough workers would be superior performers; most would be middle of the road contributors, and a few would turn out to be below average or worse on-the-job.

Prior to the Great Recession, such a normal distribution was acceptable to employers. Today, it isn't. Today, the threat from global competition and the unrelenting demands of consumers and shareholders are forcing employers to look for people who are better than good enough. They need to hire a workforce that isn't normal, but is extraordinary instead.

If you have any doubt about that, consider this. The staffing firm Veritude did a survey of employers during the last recession and found that 63 percent – better than six-out-of-ten – were using the downturn to "trade up." They were laying off those they saw as average or "C" level performers and recruiting for those who looked like "A" level workers.

Nobody told those in job market about this change. Employers didn't announce it in the media or advertise it on their corporate Web-sites. They just started hiring differently, and millions of people have been caught off guard. The rules of the game changed, yet most job seekers are still think the old rules are in effect.

How Can You Protect Yourself?

To achieve success in today's job market, you have to transform yourself from being good enough to being better than that. You must look so good to employers that they feel they have to hire you. You need to convince them that you do extraordinary work and will, therefore, make a greater than normal contribution on-the-job.

How can you accomplish that transformation? The following steps will get you started.

Step 1. Be honest with yourself.

Surveys show that we humans seriously overrate how good we really are. Most people, for example, rank themselves far higher than their supervisors do in their annual performance review. Now granted, many managers aren't especially good at making such evaluations either, but that doesn't mean we're right and they're wrong.

How can you get an accurate assessment of just how good you are (or aren't)? Ask one or both of two kinds of people:

- a former boss with whom you have stayed in contact;

or

- a former colleague who is or was also a very good friend.

Your goal in this interaction is to identify gaps in your qualifications (i.e., your performance, experience or capabilities) that make you look no better than good enough to employers. So, prepare yourself to listen without getting defensive and to learn from what you hear.

Step 2. Do something about what you learn.

Historically, the most successful people in any field have seen themselves as a work-in-progress. The all stars in professional sports, for example, never stop practicing their game. They are always trying to improve. And that's exactly what you should do, as well. The only way to be better than qualified is to be getting better all of the time.

Continuous self-improvement doesn't work, however, if it's treated like a New Year's resolution. It can't be something that you start with the best of intentions and then set aside in the press of dealing with other requirements – like a full time job or a job search. If you're going to be better than qualified and appear that way to employers, you have to:

- stick with it, so you truly are a work-in-progress;

and

- stick it on your resume, so employers will see your progress.

The new rules of the game are different, to be sure, and like anything else you're doing for the first time, they will probably take some getting used to. Once you're past that initial discomfort, however, those changes will become second nature. And when that happens, you'll find yourself always being better than you were and more than qualified for the job you want.

Tiger Job Seekers

There's been a lot of debate recently about the phenomenon of "tiger moms." While the call for tougher parenting may be controversial, however, it does raise an interesting idea. In this job market, in this economy, maybe what we need is tougher job seeking. Maybe, the key to success is to refashion ourselves as "tiger job seekers."

A tiger mom believes that she is teaching her kids critical life skills and values. While much of the media has focused on her instructional methods – the punishments and deprivations – it's the knowledge and habits she's conveying that are important to her. They are, she is convinced, the keys to a meaningful and rewarding life in the demanding new culture of the 21st Century.

Tiger job seekers don't teach others these skills and values, but instead, adopt them as their own. Their goal, however, is identical to that of tiger moms. They don't expect to use their expertise once or twice – the conventional view of job search techniques. Instead, they believe these skills and values are the keys to a successful career in the ever changing economy of the 21st Century.

What are the habits and values of a tiger mom? There are more than a few, but among the most important are:

- A belief in the importance of hard work;

- An expectation of excellence in every pursuit;

- A commitment to personal responsibility;

and

- The conviction that learning is critically important and never stops.

Let's look at each of these and see how they might apply to the tiger job seeker.

The Importance of Hard Work

A tiger mom believes success is only achieved with determined effort. A tiger job seeker invests the same commitment in their job search. For example, just as a tiger mom expects their child to forego play until their homework is done, the tiger job seeker considers their job search a full time activity. They work relentlessly to make and leverage contacts, research employers and uncover employment opportunities, apply for openings and build their personal brand. They stay at it when they're tired as well as when they're fresh, when they're discouraged as well as when they're up, and on weekends and holidays as well as during the normal business day.

An Expectation of Excellence in Every Pursuit

A tiger mom holds her kids to a very high standard in everything they do. A tiger job seeker holds themselves to a similar benchmark in the way they practice their job search. For example, just as a tiger mom expects her child to practice a piano piece until it's perfect, the tiger job seeker practices the art of networking until they master it. Whether they're an introvert or an extrovert, they work continuously to perfect their ability to build professional relationships both with their peers and prospective bosses. They learn the best practices for expanding and reinforcing their contacts and use them effectively at both meetings in the real world and in discussion forums on the Web.

A Commitment to Personal Responsibility

A tiger mom encourages her kids to take responsibility for achieving their dreams. A tiger job seeker believes it's up to them to determine the outcome of their job search. For example, just as a tiger mom will get a tutor for their child but expects the child to do their homework, a tiger job seeker is proactive about acquiring the assistance of counselors and colleagues, but accepts that it's their job to put themselves back to work. Hard as it is to do in this economy, they hold themselves accountable for the outcome of their effort and will make whatever adjustments they must to optimize their chances of success. If that means moving outside their comfort zone or making a change in what they've always done to find a job, that's exactly what they'll do.

The Conviction That Learning is Critically Important and Never Stops

A tiger mom expects her kids to acquire the habit of learning and practice it continuously. A tiger job seeker sees it as their job to transform themselves into someone employers always want to hire. For example, just as a tiger mom urges her child to explore music or the arts to express their talent, a tiger job seeker constantly strives both to increase the depth of their knowledge in their profession, craft or trade and to add ancillary skills that will enable them to use that core expertise in a wide range of situations and circumstances. They are the person whose resume details a track record of continuous development and an entry which indicates that, even while they are in transition, they are still acquiring new skills or refreshing old ones.

Regardless of what you think of a tiger mom's approach to parenting, the skills and values she inculcates in her kids will go a long way toward helping them overcome challenges and succeed in life. To overcome challenges and succeed in today's job market, those in transition would do well to adopt the same skills and values and transform themselves into tiger job seekers.

The 50-50 Job Search

The conventional wisdom is that searching for a job is, itself, a full time job. That was good advice in the 20th Century. Today, it's a formula for long term unemployment. If you spend all of your time looking for a new position, you can't get to the other task that's required to be successful in the job market. What's that? Revitalizing your career.

No one would argue that finding a job is easy, especially in today's era of cramped opportunities. It takes long hours and a lot of hard work to research employers, reply to their ads and network with friends and colleagues. In the past, however, you could also be certain that such dedication would pay off in a reasonably short period of time. In weeks or at most a month or two, you would have a couple of job offers, and one would probably be better than the last job you had.

That's no longer true. In this tepid recovery, you can exert the same level of effort you did in the past and still come up short. You can even work harder than you did in your last job search and still find yourself without an offer. Why? Because employers have changed the rules of the game. They're no longer looking for qualified applicants for their openings. They want to hire the "better than qualified" person.

How can you make yourself look like a better than qualified person? That's where the 50-50 job search comes in. You spend half your time working as hard as you can on your job search and the other half of your time transforming yourself into a candidate that employers simply can't resist.

How Do You Become Irresistible to Employers?

In today's tough economy, businesses are looking to draw as much talent and productivity as possible out of each employee. You can argue about the fairness of the increased requirements but not about the reality of their existence. Employers want their workers to be:

- at the state-of-the-art in their profession, craft or trade;

and

- able to contribute continuously to their success in a significant way.

Everybody claims to have those traits, so simply saying that you do isn't enough. You have to prove that you are a better than qualified person, and that takes three steps.

Step 1: Candidly assess the status of your qualifications. As a minimum, ask yourself these questions:

- When was the last time you took an in-depth course in the latest tools and techniques used in your field? If the answer is more than a year ago, you're not a better than qualified prospect.

- Have you ever acquired skills that would expand the range of situations in which you could contribute to your employer? Do you speak a second language, for example, or do you know how to use the latest technology in your industry? If the answer is no, you're not a better than qualified prospect.

Step 2. Plug the gaps in your qualifications, beginning with those that are most likely to be of concern to employers.

If you're uncertain of the priorities, ask a couple of hiring managers in your field. As a general rule, however, always begin by remediating any deficiencies in your primary field and then work on adding complementary skills that will make you even more able to contribute.

There are, of course, a range of alternatives you can use in this effort. Check out:

- Local community colleges,

- The programs offered by your professional or trade association, and

- Online courses from training firms and academic institutions.

Step 3. Promote your effort.

Don't wait until you're done with your educational effort and don't assume that recruiters and hiring managers will know to ask about it. Start getting the word out the minute you start to get better than qualified.

Add your coursework to your LinkedIn profile and Facebook page if you have them. Do an email blast to update friends and colleagues. And, of course, make sure you feature the skills you're acquiring on your resume.

I realize that some people are uncomfortable with such self-promotion. But, as an old mentor of mine once opined, "It ain't braggin' if ya' done it." A thoughtfully crafted update on your occupational credentials will help to reposition you in the job market. It'll set you apart from others and make you all but irresistible to employers.

The Application Two-Step

Here's a common scenario that's playing out on the Internet today: you spend hours surfing the Web and visiting job boards; you search through hundreds of job postings in their job databases; and finally, you find what you've been looking for. There, right in front of you, is an opening that matches your qualifications perfectly. So, what do you do? Send in your resume, right? Well, not exactly. If that's all it took, a lot more people would be getting offers and starting out at new jobs.

In today's Mad Hatter job market, you can't get a job by applying for it. You have to do more. You have to apply not once, but twice in a process I call the Application Two-Step.

- Step 1 is a test.

- Step 2 is the answer.

Perform the first step, and you will be considered an applicant; perform the second, and you will be noticed. Perform both steps, and you will likely move to the head of the applicant line.

Step 1: The Test

A job posting is a test. Its purpose is to determine whether or not you paid attention in Mrs. Murphy's kindergarten class. What was the first lesson you were taught there? That's right: you must follow directions. So, a job posting is, first and foremost, a test to determine whether you can submit your application according to the employer's instructions.

It might tell you to:

- Cut and paste your resume into an online application form;

- Cut and paste your resume into a regular, old e-mail message;

- Send your resume as an attachment to an e-mail message; or

- Send your resume to the employer by old fashioned postal mail.

Whatever the method that's specified, the key to being considered a bona fide applicant is to do exactly as you are instructed. It doesn't matter if it's easier or more convenient for you to do something else. Step 1 is a pass or fail exam; either you follow the employer's directions and are thus worthy of consideration or you don't and are considered a "graffiti applicant" who belongs in the reject pile.

Step 2: The Answer

If Step 1 enables you to pass the test; Step 2 provides the answer that will ace it. As soon as you have positioned yourself as a bona fide applicant, you must reposition your resume to make sure it gets priority attention.

Recruiters are inundated with applicant resumes these days, so it's very hard for any single person – even one who is extremely qualified for an opening – to get noticed. To overcome that disadvantage, therefore, you must help your resume stand out. And, the best way to do that is by networking.

You have plenty of resources at your disposal, but the best for this kind of rapid networking are online. They include your connections on LinkedIn and other social media sites, your college or university alumni organization, and the discussion forum on the Web-site of your professional or trade association. Use every single one of them to find one (or both) of two kinds of contacts:

- An employee of the organization whom you know.

- An employee whom you don't know, but with whom you share an affinity (e.g., you have the same professional affiliation or a common alma mater).

Once you've made a connection, reach out to the person and ask them to pass your resume along to the appropriate recruiter in their HR Department. If that happens, your resume will move from being just one more among the hundreds or thousands in the organization's resume database to being one of a handful or less on the recruiter's desktop. At that point, the odds are far, far greater that it and you will get the consideration you deserve.

Applying for a job online just isn't as simple as it might at first seem. In fact, the process is actually both the first assessment an employer will make of your capabilities as a prospective employee and the single best way to make sure that your resume gets looked at first by recruiters. And, the secret to passing the test and then acing it is to practice the Application Two-Step.

The Secret to an Effective Resume

If you've been in the world of work for more than 15 minutes, you know just how uncommunicative a resume is. No matter how much information you cram into that document, it simply cannot convey the character, dedication or capability you offer to an employer. You can, however, remedy this situation, but you'll have to accept a counter-intuitive idea to do so.

The secret to creating an effective resume is to throw out the conventional approach to that document and use a new one – one that's best described as an "incomplete record." Ironically, presenting an incomplete portrait of yourself is the only way you can look better than the rest of the crowd in today's job market.

Despite its name, the "incomplete record" has all of the information provided by a traditional resume. It is a detailed description of your work experience and accomplishments, your education and training, and your professional or occupational affiliations and activities (e.g., the associations to which you belong). This self-description must tell employers what you can do, of course, but equally as important, it must also tell them what kind of contribution you can make to their success.

The information can also be presented in any one of the traditional formats for a resume: chronological, functional or hybrid. The only difference in an "incomplete record" is at the beginning of the document. Regardless of the format you select, the resume must begin with an Accomplishments Summary that appears directly beneath your name and contact information. This three-to-four line section should use keywords and phrases to highlight your strongest credentials for employment. It ensures that recruiters will see your best assets, even if they don't read all or even most of your resume.

At a superficial level, therefore, the "incomplete record" looks just like any other resume. So, what makes it incomplete? You do.

In order for a resume to be an "incomplete record," you must first become incomplete yourself. You see, employers face two certainties in the 21st Century workplace:

- *Certainty 1:* The skills that are necessary to make a meaningful contribution on-the-job today will be different from those required to make a commensurate contribution tomorrow.

and

- *Certainty 2:* Employers no longer have the resources or the time to provide the development necessary to keep workers up-to-date with their skills.

As a result, every organization now needs workers who get it and get it done on their own.

Proving That You Get It & Get It Done On Your Own

An "incomplete record" is designed to prove to employers that you understand the certainties of the modern workplace. You design your resume to acknowledge – and promote the fact – that you are an incomplete professional in your field and that you take personal responsibility for fixing that situation. In other words, you don't want the document to perform as a traditional resume and show you as a completed person, but instead, to convey exactly the opposite impression. You use it to promote yourself as proudly unfinished in your development.

How Do You Do That?

One way is to add a new entry after each job you describe in the Experience section of your resume. It should begin with the phrase "What I learned" and conclude with a list of the key insights and wisdom you acquired through your employment.

Another way is to start upgrading your skills right now. Even if you're already an expert in your field. And, even if you're in an active job search. Enroll in an educational or training program that will strengthen your ability to contribute on-the-job. Everyone can get better at what they do, and pursuing that self-improvement is the only way to protect yourself from the never ending creep of obsolescence in the modern workplace.

Then, add that credential to your record. First, make yourself look incomplete by adding the following information to the Education section of your resume:

- The name of the course or program you're taking;

- The institution or organization that's providing it;

- The term *Ongoing.*

Then, add a key phrase denoting that effort to your Accomplishments Summary. Why? Because improving yourself is an accomplishment.

Those simple entries will convey a powerful message to any prospective employer. It signals that you know you can always get smarter in your field and that you take personal responsibility for doing so. It shows you have the humility to acknowledge what you don't know and the courage to add to what you do know. There's no more appealing credential to an employer in today's job market, and only the "incomplete record" enables you to claim it.

The One Word You Should Avoid in a Job Search

In today's highly competitive job market, the worst word you can use is "can." I realize that's a stunning turn of events for a people who have historically seen themselves as the "can do" nation. Nevertheless, what employers now want from candidates is a verb they believe has far greater potential. The word they want to hear is "will."

Until recently, employers competed in a global marketplace on the basis of productivity. The more efficient a company's workers, the more profitable it would be. That strategy unfolded in three distinct phases.

First, employers outsourced jobs to cheaper labor overseas. Then, they turned to technology to replace humans on-the-job. And finally, for the past decade or so, they've relied on the pernicious notion of "doing more with less" to squeeze ever more profits out of the workforce left behind.

This quest for productivity is now coming to an end. There are no more costs to be squeezed out of the organization, technology has reached its upper limits of capability at least for the moment, and employees are just too exhausted to give any more.

And, at the very same time, there is a new and formidable dynamic emerging in the global marketplace. It is the *globalization of genius*. We are now competing with many more smart people around the world. And, that reality is changing what employers want and need from you.

Playing the Big A

Early in the movie *The Social Network*, Mark Zuckerberg is trying to impress his date with how smart he is. At one point, he says, "There are more geniuses in China than the entire population of the U.S." He, of course, thinks he is similarly endowed with a high IQ, and that smart people have a competitive advantage in the global marketplace.

They don't. What counts in economic competition is not your IQ, but your talent. And, talent is a universal donor. We all have it. It is an attribute of our species.

You see, talent is not an exceptional skill – it is not the ability to win The X Factor or the World Series – it is the *capacity for excellence*. And excellence is what employers want and need from their employees.

How does that change the way you compete for a job?

Your resume, your interview, your conversations with the recruiter – all of those interactions – must make a very different case from that which you made to land your last job. In the past, you simply had to prove you <u>can</u> do the work. Today, you must prove you <u>will</u> excel at it.

How do you accomplish that?

Take every opportunity to recount not what you did, but rather, how well you did it. I call this "playing the Big A" – your accomplishments on-the-job. What's an accomplishment? It's an outcome or result you achieved that <u>helped your employer be more successful</u>.

For example:

- Make sure your resume features your accomplishments in previous jobs. Recruiters are busy, however, and may not read through the entire document, so place an Accomplishments Summary (not a Skills Summary) right at the top where they'll be sure to see it.

- If you have a profile on LinkedIn or a Facebook page, revise it to highlight your accomplishments at work. Be careful, however, to set the right tone. You're not bragging about what you did, but celebrating how you contributed to your employer.

- Rehearse the description of your key accomplishment in previous jobs before you go into an interview. Make sure you can clearly and succinctly articulate how your actions directly and meaningfully accrued to your employer's advantage.

Global competition has shifted from a quest for productivity to a search for talent. In order to succeed, therefore, employers no longer need candidates who can do a job. They are, instead, desperate to hire those who will excel at their work. Focus your job search on proving you have that qualification and you'll be competitive every time you apply for an opening.

A "Perfect" Stranger

Think about it this way. A person you've never met – a connection through a friend of a friend – emails you out of the blue to request that you send a copy of their resume to your HR Department. They explain that they are applying for a job with your employer and would like some help. It's a simple request, so would you do it?

What this person is asking makes a lot of sense, especially in these days and times. They want to stand out from the crowd. There's just one problem – they don't stand out in your mind. You have no idea who they are. So, their request isn't as simple as it first appears to be. They want you to take the time and assume the risk of passing along the resume of a "perfect" stranger.

Now granted, your time investment may, at least at first blush, seem trivial. All you have to do is forward their message (and attached resume) on to someone in HR. But still, they've interrupted your train of thought, and that act has a cost that is greater than you may realize. Research now shows that it typically takes a person about 25 minutes to get back on track when they are interrupted by an outside com-munication. Add that to the time you take to read their request, track down the right email address in the HR Department and pass along the message, and you've probably invested a fair amount of your workday in someone you don't even know.

Remember What Your Mother Taught You

The greater threat, however, is the risk you assume by implicitly endorsing the person you send on to the HR Department. Even if you add a caveat in your message indicating that you don't know this individual from Adam or Eve, you have gone to the trouble of referring them, and that step is a real, if subtle, form of recommendation.

Of course, the devil-may-care among us will shrug and say so what. The more careful in the crowd, however, will worry about what this "perfect" stranger (implicitly) says about you. After all, the caliber of both their qualifications and the character they display are a reflection on the friends and connections you keep – even if you are separated by two or even three degrees. Sure, it would be nice to help this person out. But, in today's tenuous employment climate, anything that might detract from your perceived stature in the organization is dangerous.

Basically, you are being asked to lend your hard-earned standing in the organization to someone you don't even know. So, think back to what your mother taught you. What was her first and most important rule? That's right. Don't speak to strangers. There was no caveat about it being O.K. to speak to strangers on the Web. Her rule was uncompromising and absolute. It is inappropriate if not downright risky to speak with (or on behalf of) someone you don't know. And, Facebook, LinkedIn and Twitter don't diminish the relevance of that dictum.

The Other Side of the Table

Now, put yourself on the other side of the table. If you're in transition and sitting at your laptop all day friending up a storm, building up connections like crazy and following like a maniac, are you doing yourself any good? It's true that you will meet lots of strangers that way, but will you interact with anyone who really cares about you? Or be willing to help you out in today's "nobody seems safe" workplace?

You see, there's a difference between superficial networking – making contact with others – and true networking – investing the time and effort to get to know them. If you would like someone to be helpful to you, you have to first commit yourself to building familiarity and trust with them. That doesn't mean tweeting about the kind of pizza you had yesterday; it means creating and then sustaining a professional relationship with them through online and, if possible, off-line interactions.

Now, if you've ever been in a relationship before, you've acquired two insights about them. First, they take serious work to develop. And second, that work takes time. What does that mean for someone in transition? Here are the hard truths about networking during a job search in today's unsettled economic environment:

- *Truth #1:* Many of those you reach out to and ask to help you, won't. They aren't being mean-spirited, but are instead, simply being careful. If you've never met and gotten to know them, you're a stranger and thus represent a risk many will feel they cannot take.

- *Truth #2:* Since it takes time to build up a relationship through networking, the time to begin is before you're in transition. Make it a priority each and every day to transform yourself from being a stranger in your field to being someone a lot of people know and respect. That's the best form of employment security you'll ever have.

- *Truth #3:* If you haven't done much if any networking in advance and find yourself in transition, look for ways to look like less of a stranger. Don't connect with any and everyone, but concentrate instead on those with whom you share an alma mater, membership in a professional association or even a non-work affiliation (e.g., participation in a veterans group or local environmental action committee). Then, invest the time and make the effort to get to know them.

Collectively, these truths confirm that what you learned as a child is still relevant and helpful now that you're an adult: the only "perfect" stranger is someone who isn't a stranger at all.

The Dilemma of a Wimpy Job Seeker

The movie, *Diary of a Wimpy Kid,* earned quick kudos for its observations of middle school and the lessons it teaches adolescents about life there and thereafter. Its wisdom, however, is not confined to pre-high school hallways. The story has something to offer to those of us who are trying to survive another hostile and seemingly incomprehensible setting – the job market.

While the wimpy kid faces cafeteria bullies and hallway brickbats, the wimpy job seeker is confronted with indifferent employers and recruiters and unanswered applications. The experiences are vastly different, but the net result is exactly the same. Both the adolescent and the adult feel as if they're being shoved around by forces they cannot control and humbled if not humiliated by their inability to defend themselves.

You'll have to see the movie to find out how the wimpy kid deals with his situation. However, for the wimpy job seekers among us – and in today's job market we all qualify to some extent for that label – the following game plan will help to provide some relief.

First, you have to think back to what your mother or father taught you about dealing with bullies. You can't run away or hide from them. The only way to deal with bullies is to face them down. Or to put it another way, you have to acquire the physical and mental strength to stand up for yourself.

How do you acquire such fortitude in today's job market? You learn and then use the principles and practices of "career fitness." Like physical fitness, it's based on two simple but powerful ideas:

- You are responsible for the health of your career, not your employer, your boss or anyone else.

and

- You have to work on building up the fitness of your career every single day, not after your job search is over.

To put it bluntly, if you're professionally flabby or a 90 pound weakling in your field, your workplace recess (or what we adults call unemployment) will continue to be torture. On the other hand, if you stick up for yourself and correct your wimpiness, you will unleash the exceptional person you have the potential to be.

The Best Way to Correct Wimpiness

Luckily, a wimpy career is not an irresolvable condition. It can be corrected. As I describe in my book, Work Strong: Your Personal Career Fitness System, what's required is the daily use of a "career fitness regimen." It covers all seven facets of a healthy career and ensures that you'll have the occupational credentials, stature and outlook for success, even in the face of a bully-like job market.

Here's a brief description of the regimen:

I. Pump Up Your Cardiovascular System
The heart of your career is your occupational expertise, not your knowledge of some employer's standard operating procedures. The pace of change, however, makes fifty percent of that expertise obsolete every twelve months. So, keep yourself relevant and respected by constantly updating and enriching your expertise.

II. Strengthen Your Circulatory System
The circulatory system of your career is your network of contacts. The wider and deeper they are, the more visible and highly regarded you are likely to be in the workplace. To achieve that recognition, however, you have to netWORK, not net-get-around-to-it-whenever-it's-convenient.

In other words, make networking an integral part of your business (and job searching) day.

III. Develop All of Your Muscle Groups
The greater your versatility in contributing your expertise at work, the broader the array of situations and assignments in which you can be employed. So, add ancillary skills (e.g., a second language, knowledge of advanced technology) that will expand where and how your core capabilities can be applied in the workplace.

IV. Increase Your Flexibility & Range of Motion
These days, career progress is not always a straight line, nor does it always look as it has in the past or stay the same for very long. So, learn the skills that will enable you to cope with and adapt to changing requirements and circumstances. They will multiply your employment opportunities and strengthen your perceived value among employers.

V. Work With Winners
Successful organizations and coworkers aid and abet your ability to accomplish your career goals, while unsupportive organizations and less capable peers diminish it. Therefore, be as selective of the employers for which you will work as they are of the workers to whom they will offer a job.

VI. Stretch Your Soul
A healthy career not only serves you, it serves others, as well. Look for ways to contribute your expertise to your community, your country or our planet. There's obviously nothing wrong with offering a strong back or financial support, but you make your greatest gift when you share your talent – your capacity for excellence – with others.

VII. Pace Yourself
A fulfilling and rewarding career depends upon your getting the rest and replenishment you need to do your best work every day you are on-the-job. Relearn the skills of planning for and actually experiencing leisure (e.g., turn off your Blackberry when you're lying on the beach) and focus on enjoying yourself and those around you.

There's much more to the Career Fitness Regimen, but this brief summary provides an outline of what it takes to correct wimpiness. As with a physical fitness program, you'll need a bit of courage to get started and a bit of determination to stick with it, but if you do, you'll see an amazing transformation in yourself. The job seeker who used to get pushed around in the job market will be replaced by a hardy individual with the strength, reach and endurance to succeed.

The Two Best Ways to Find a Job All-in-One

A recent survey of 200 large employers in the U.S. identified the top two ways they recruited new employees. Number one was referrals; number two was job boards. Between them, those two sources accounted for over half of the people the organizations hired in 2010. While these findings are helpful, however, they also raise two important questions: First, how do you find out which job boards employers are using and second, how do you make referrals work for you?

The Best Job Boards for You

There are over 100,000 job boards now operating on the Web. Collectively, they post over two million job openings each and every day. That's a lot of opportunity, but it can also be a bit overwhelming. How do you figure out which job boards will work best for you?

Most of us know the largest and most famous of those sites – Monster and CareerBuilder.com. They provide access to job openings in virtually every profession, craft and trade and in every location on the planet. Other sites such as Indeed and Simply Hired aggregate job postings from a number of sites and then link you back to them for application. And finally, there are tens of thousands of niche or specialty sites that focus on a particular occupation, industry, geographic location or affinity. They range from AllRetailJobs.com, a site for all kinds of positions in the retail industry, to VetJobs.com, a site for military personnel transitioning into the private sector.

All of these sites post job ads, but no one site can connect you with all of the employers posting jobs or to all of the jobs they are posting online. For that reason, you have to use a number of sites to optimize your access to the openings employers are currently trying to fill. I suggest you use an approach I call the *5:1 Method*. It looks like this: 2GP + 3N = 1GJ.

The 2GP stands for two general purpose sites. They give you the broadest possible access to the right job openings for you. These sites could be Monster and CareerBuilder.com or any of the dozens of other sites that post recruitment ads in a wide cross section of career fields, industries and locations.

The 3N stands for three niche sites. They give you the deepest possible access to job postings in the workplace. Pick one site that specializes in your career field, one that focuses on your industry, and one that serves the geographic area where you live or want to work.

And finally, the 1GJ stands for one great job. If you pick the right five sites and visit them regularly, you will dramatically increase your chances of finding the one great job for you.

How can you determine which sites to use? Check with friends and colleagues to see which sites they've found worked best. If you can, talk to a recruiter or hiring manager in your field or industry and get their recommendations. If you're feeling adventurous, use Google, Yahoo! or Bing to do your own research online. And finally, of course, you can tap into the research that's already been done and published in books and other references, including *WEDDLE's Guide to Employment Sites on the Internet*.

The Application Two-Step

Once you've found the five best sites for your job search, the next step is to use them effectively. Unfortunately, most job seekers think that you use a job board today the same way you did before the recession. You don't.

Our slow-moving recovery has meant that a job posting now generates dozens, sometimes hundreds and occasionally even a thousand or more applications. If all you do is hit the Apply button, therefore, the chances are high that you will be lost in the herd, even if you are well qualified for the opening.

What's the alternative? Practice the Application Two-Step.

Step 1:

First, prove that you care enough to invest some time in your application. Never submit a generic resume, but instead, always tailor your resume to the specific requirements of the opening. Second, prove that you can follow directions. Submit your resume exactly as instructed in the job posting. If the ad says to attach it, don't embed it in an email message. If it says to embed the document, don't attach it. Recruiters are typically juggling a number of openings at any one time, so they have no time or patience for anyone who colors outside the lines.

Step 2:

Since your application will inevitably be one of many, immediately begin networking to find one of two kinds of people who have a very specific attribute: they are someone you know or someone with whom you share an affinity (e.g., you both are members of the same professional association or graduated from the same college) and they work at the organization with the opening. Reach out to them and ask if they will walk your resume into the HR Department and refer you to the recruiter who's working on it. That referral will virtually guarantee that your resume will be reviewed and your candidacy seriously considered.

In today's job market, the key to success is optimizing what you do and how you do it. You want to maximize your effectiveness while minimizing any inefficiencies in the process. Or, to put it another way, you should use the two best ways to find a job all-in-one.

What General Petraeus Can Teach Job Seekers

In 2005, General David Petraeus was an executive in transition. Having fallen out of favor with the civilian leadership in the Department of Defense, he was reassigned to lead the Army's mid-level leadership school in Fort Leavenworth, Kansas. For a combat commander, that wasn't a lateral move, it was a big step backwards. What the General did next, however, provides a rich case study of how to recover from a career setback.

Given his current high regard in both the media and the government, it's easy to forget that General Petraeus was an outsider looking in late in his career. How did he accomplish this extraordinary transformation? He followed a game plan that every single person who is out of work and feeling out of luck can and should emulate. It involves just three steps:

- Reinvigorate your talent

- Redefine your brand

- Stay true to your new you.

Let's take a brief look at each of them.

Reinvigorate Your Talent

General Petraeus had spent his entire career as an infantryman. He was a proud, old fashioned rifle carrying soldier whose job was to defeat the enemy in close combat. That's what he had been trained to do and that's certainly what he knew how to do best. It was not, however, what the Army needed for the war in Iraq. It had won the war with the Iraqi Army, but it was losing the insurgency that followed it.

So, what did General Petraeus do? First, he carefully assessed the situation on the ground in Iraq to determine what the problem was. Then, he thought through the alternative strategies and determined that the traditional tactics of ground combat had to be replaced with a new kind of counterinsurgency warfare. Finally, he acquired the knowledge necessary to develop that new strategy and literally wrote the book – the Army's Field Manual – which detailed it.

That's exactly what those of us in transition need to be doing, as well. Employers increasingly believe they need new strategies and tactics to win the competition in the global marketplace. They are no longer looking for people who can perform the job the way it used to be done – no matter how well they were able to do it. What they want, what they need, is someone who can devise new approaches to performing work and is willing to extend their talent so they can deliver those approaches effectively on-the-job. You don't have to write a book, but you do have to be credibly able to deliver innovative excellence on-the-job.

Redefine Your Brand

General Petraeus didn't just develop a new way of war-fighting, he redefined himself as its author and champion. In other words, he was no longer an old fashioned infantryman; he was the "father of counter-insurgency" and rebuilt his reputation on that theme. He was tireless in his efforts to explain it to his superiors in the Defense Department, to convert his peers to his point of view and to convince all of them of its potential to turn the tide in Iraq.

A similar campaign is also critical to success for those of us in transition. Hard as it is to reshape your talent for the new and often confusing needs of the post recession world of work, that's only half the battle. Once you've accomplished your reinvigoration, you have to convince others that you're different. You have to break out of your legacy brand – the old way you described yourself in the workforce – and develop a clear and compelling description of your new persona.

This redefined brand must be accurate, of course, but beyond, that it must set you apart. It must differentiate you from those who are still offering the conventional strategies and tactics in your field and for the kind of job you seek. And, it has to portray you as the singular person who both knows how to be a key contributor to the success of an employer and will not flinch from playing that role.

Stay True to Your New You

The journey of General Petraeus from a backwater command in Kansas to the front lines of this nation's Armed Forces (and now, the head of the CIA) didn't occur without some difficult twists in the road and a setback or two. He had the courage of his convictions, however, and a fierce determination to succeed. He fought through the hard times because he believed in himself and what he could do. While his reinvigorated talent and redefined brand were both essential to his advancement, it was that factor – his character – which ensured his success.

The same is true for those of us in the civilian workplace. Whether you've been shoved out the door and into the job market or into a box with no security or opportunity, it is who you are on the inside that will determine what happens to you on the outside. That doesn't mean the course will be easy or without its frustrations, but it does mean there is hope ... if you believe enough in yourself to grab hold of it.

Not everyone can lead an army into combat but everyone – every single person – can be a victor even in today's rough and tumble world of work. It will require that you teach your talent some new and more powerful ways of contributing and that you reset your brand so that your new capability is recognized by prospective employers. Those tasks take courage and commitment, to be sure, but their accomplish-ment is a gift, an affirmation of the indomitable spirit resident in each and all of us. If you stay true to that limitless personal possibility, you will always end up a winner.

Section II:
How to Hang Onto
Your Job
in a Turbulent
Workplace

What You Need to Know First: What the Post-Recession Workplace is Actually Like

Articles in This Section

NOTES

Land of the Free and Home of the Brave

Time magazine once featured Jonathan Franzen, the author of the novel *Freedom*, on its cover. Though I've not read the book, its title got me to thinking about the liberty we enjoy in the United States of America. Historically, we have imagined ourselves to be the "land of the free and home of the brave," but are we? When it comes to our careers, at least, I think we're still a work-in-progress.

Freedom is a noun, but it can only be achieved with a verb. In other words, freedom doesn't exist unless and until we act to be free. We can live in the United States of America where we have a right to freedom, but we can easily become prisoners of our assumptions and beliefs.

Many people, for example, assumed that there would always be a CompUSA, Enron and Lehman Brothers so they lashed their careers to those employers. They didn't exercise their freedom – they hunkered down and hung on – and saw themselves locked into a downward spiral of missed opportunities that resulted in unemployment. They assumed that someone else would steer them toward success, and discovered too late that only they themselves can do that.

That's the central paradox of freedom in the workplace. We are free to act in our careers, but freedom doesn't actually occur until we do. To put it another way, freedom isn't free. It is earned by the effort we make to select and pursue our own destiny at work. And, that's where freedom gets tough. It's hard to figure out which field will provide us with a rewarding and fulfilling career, and it's just as difficult to ensure we're continuously qualified for employment in that field.

Instinctively, we already know that. It's why we say we're the "land of the free <u>and</u> the home of the brave." Only a courageous person can be free. Every American has a right to freedom, but only those who are brave enough to exercise that right will ever achieve it.

The United States of America didn't happen because the Founding Fathers recognized peoples' legitimate access to Life, Liberty and the pursuit of Happiness. It happened because they acknowledged those rights <u>and</u> declared our Independence. Those rights, and especially Liberty, became a reality because a bunch of brave colonists used a verb to create them.

An Example Worth Emulating

The Founding Fathers were extraordinary people, to be sure, but they were also citizens of this Republic just like you and me. They were smart, but not geniuses, so sometimes they made mistakes. They were clear thinking, but not omniscient, so sometimes they were blindsided by the consequences of their decisions. They were, in short, brave but human. And that means, we can emulate their actions.

We can live and work to their standards. We too can show the courage necessary to achieve freedom, to be free. How does that happen in a 21st Century career? Here are some examples that will point you in the right direction:

- *According to the U.S. Labor Department, between February and April of 2010, more people resigned from their jobs (2 million) than were laid off (1.7 million).* They had the courage to take their career into their own hands and chart a course that made more sense for them. They exercised their freedom, even in the teeth of a stuttering economy.

- *According to the U.S. Department of Education, 92 million American adults are now enrolled in an education program.* That's over half of the workforce. These working men and women are brave enough to take personal responsibility for their own development. They are exercising their freedom by reinforcing their ability to perform at their peak on-the-job.

- *According to Time magazine, 40 million Americans move each year and 20 percent of them do so in order to take a new job.* They are courageous enough to head off into the frontier of a new locale in order to stake their claim to a better future for themselves and their family. They have earned their freedom by overcoming their fear of the unknown.

It is possible, of course, to be free without quitting your job or going back to school or moving to a new town. There is a common denominator in all of those examples, however. It is individual initiative. And, you cannot be free without that personal expression of bravery.

Freedom is a quintessential American ideal, but it is also one that is often misunderstood. We think we are free because we live in a free society. And while that is certainly our good fortune, it is not how freedom happens. True freedom – the independence to reach for and become the epitome of ourselves – only occurs if we are daring enough to set ourselves free.

The War for Work

The Great Recession changed everything. The workplace was being pushed and shoved in new directions long before 2008, but that economic cataclysm brought all those forces to a head. And now, we have a very different reality from that which existed just a few short years ago. Today, we are embroiled in a War for Work.

Although the menace of terrorism is still real and proximate, we are now facing a new challenge that poses an even greater threat to our way of life. It's not far away in Iraq or Afghanistan; it's in Boston and Cleveland and Phoenix and Los Angeles too.

This situation endangers our ability both to create a comfortable standard of living for ourselves and to pass along an even better tomorrow to our kids. To put it bluntly (and without any exaggeration), the War for Work is an all out attack on the American Dream. And, it's happening right here at home.

Unlike our struggle with terrorism, however, this assault is not being perpetrated by an obvious and evil enemy. In fact, the aggressors are benign. Their actions are legal and not all that dissimilar from our own. With some obvious exceptions, we are under attack by people who have adopted our creed. By working hard, by doing skilled work, by making a real contribution, by applying new and better ideas, they are stealing our future. They are replacing the American Dream with the Chinese Dream and the German Dream and the Indian Dream.

If you have any doubt about the seriousness of this threat – if you think I'm exaggerating – look around you. One-out-of-five Americans is unemployed, under-employed or without hope. Millions more come to work each morning not knowing if they'll have a job by the end of the day. People don't even talk about job security anymore; no one wants to indulge in fantasy when their reality is so frightful.

How Do We Defend Ourselves?

Here's the hard truth. You can't win the War for Work – you won't be able to hang onto your job – by simply doing what you have always done at work. I know that's not what you'd like to hear, but it's the truth. That approach was effective in a time of peace. In a time of war, it isn't enough.

What should we do? How can we protect ourselves from this threat to our way of life? If there's no defense in what we are doing – if working harder and putting in more hours won't keep us employed – what else is there?

The place to begin, I believe, is on the inside. If we want to strengthen our defenses and steel ourselves for victory in the War for Work, we have to change our values. We have to discard the self-delusion that employment is somehow guaranteed in the United States of America or that the job we have today will always be there for us tomorrow. We must jettison the self-indulgence of assuming that our competence at work will somehow magically stay at the level it needs to be.

If we want to preserve and protect our ability to work – if we want to win the War for Work and save the American Dream – we're going to have to adopt the values of victory. And who better to learn those values from than the Greatest Generation? They sacrificed in the near term to ensure our longer term security. They didn't expect success to be handed to them; they were ready and willing to work hard for it. They were self-reliant, self-motivated and fearless.

And, that's what we need to be, as well. We have to set our sights on becoming the Greater-than-the-Greatest Generation. They were im- perfect, to be sure, but they were also exemplars of the work ethic and quiet sense of duty that made this country such a special place. So, it's entirely appropriate that we should both emulate and do our best to improve on their outlook, their beliefs, and their commitments.

Ironically, that's exactly what they would want. They were the Americans who showed the courage, the tenacity and the generosity of spirit to give their kids a better future. They would be proud to have us do the same. And, do so even better.

The Punishing Power of Parity

Sports enthusiasts know the term well. "Parity" describes a situation in which opposing teams have relatively equal capabilities. When it occurs, no team – not even the previous year's champion – has a competitive advantage. Victory is determined by hard-to-predict intangibles. On the playing field and in the global marketplace.

When sports teams are at parity, talent no longer sets the outcome of the game. That turn of events may make for more enjoyable viewing by the fans, but it's very tough on the teams. In essence, they no longer control their destiny. Winning isn't based on the skills of the players, but on such factors as the environment – whether it's snowing and below zero or sunny and warm – and luck – which players are injured and how badly.

The same is true of corporate competitors. When there is parity among workers' skills, no company can dominate the marketplace. Instead, victory depends on such intangibles as cost – who will work for less – and luck – which government sets the best commercial policy. And, that's precisely the situation that now exists in the global economy.

Companies in China, Japan, Germany and India have brought the talent of their teams up to the level of America's workers. Today, the manufacturing, mechanical, programming, accounting, customer service and other skills in those countries are every bit as good as (and, in some cases, better than) the skills of our workers here in the U.S. of A.. To put it bluntly, we've lost our competitive edge.

That message is tough to accept when you've spent your entire career in a global economy dominated by American companies and their employees. Nevertheless, it's true. We haven't gotten worse; the competition has gotten better. As a consequence, we and the rest of the world are now at parity.

So, what's to be done?

Well, basically, we have only two choices: We can hope that the fickle finger of fate treats us kindly or we can take matters into our own hands.

Self-Reliance as a Self-Preservation Strategy

America's corporate employers have already made their choice. They've decided to set a new course. They are determined to break out of the shackles of parity by recruiting more of the top talent in the work-force. In fact, as they see it, they are now in a War for Talent, where the winners will be those organizations that acquire an unfair share of the highest performing employees.

How should you respond?

Take matters into your own hands and take advantage of this extraordi-nary pent-up demand for talent. Make self-reliance your self-preserva-tion strategy.

- Whether you've always been a top performer or done just enough to get by, remake yourself into a "worker in progress." Build continu-ous self-improvement into your normal business day.

and

- Whether you're looking to excel in your current job or preparing to move to a better one, make personal development an integral part of your strategy. Take proactive steps to upgrade, expand, refine and reinvigorate your skill set and get started right away.

Why go to all that trouble?

Because rising above the common denominator of parity is the only way to ensure employment in the 21st Century world of work. Cheap labor can't win when the alternative is better talent.

The Hidden Deficit in Your Career

Everyone in America is in debt. If you've been prudent and kept your finances in order, your government hasn't. That reality means all of us are in hock. Unfortunately, however, that's not the only deficit we're dealing with. Many of us are now also debtors in our careers. Our occupational knowledge is nearly or already bankrupt.

Historically, working Americans have relied on two kinds of knowledge in the workplace: occupational and experiential. We went to school and attended training programs to keep ourselves up-to-date in our field of work, and we learned the practical lessons of how things actually got done and done well through our day-to-day interactions on-the-job.

While both of those kinds of knowledge were deemed important, they were not given equal weight, either in our own minds or in those of our employers. Book learning was obviously an important foundation, but the superstructure of experience was the gold standard of an employee's value. Indeed, until recently, if there was a choice between two candidates, one with the latest knowledge and no experience and one with slightly (or even significantly) dated expertise and a lot of experience, most organizations would have opted for the person with the longer track record.

Moreover, if you've been in the workforce for more than five years, you probably came to rely on that approach to worker valuation. Sure, you tended to your occupational knowledge, but you did so episodically and at a relatively leisurely pace. It was an effective strategy for managing your career because occupational knowledge expanded and was refined at a similarly slow rate. As a result, your mastery in your field had a long half-life.

Today, it doesn't.

The Shorter Half-Life of Occupational Knowledge

The half-life of occupational knowledge has shrunk dramatically in the last decade. The pace of new knowledge creation and old knowledge obsolescence has now accelerated in every career field. It doesn't matter whether you're a salesperson who must stay abreast of a constantly changing array of new products or a systems analyst who must be conversant in a continuously expanding universe of new software, half of your expertise is now obsolete every twelve months.

What does that mean for you and your career? To put it bluntly, you are going to have to acknowledge one change and make another.

First, you must now accept that the relative importance of expertise and experience has shifted.

Employers now view your expertise as more critical to their success than your experience. They believe they need state-of-the-art knowledge in order to compete in the global marketplace. Experience is still obviously helpful and remains an important criterion for high performance. But, it is the contemporaneity of your knowledge about concepts, techniques, technologies and products or services in your field that will enable you to make a meaningful contribution on-the-job.

Second, you can no longer afford to coast in your occupational development.

There is no recess when it comes to staying current in your field. You must now be in school all of the time – when you're employed and even when you're not. That self-improvement should always focus first on your core expertise – your skills and knowledge in your career field – and then expand out to give you ancillary skills. Those skills are "contribution multipliers." They either increase the range of situations and circumstances in which you can be employed or they expand the impact of your performance on-the-job.

These two shifts have introduced a simple but powerful new key to success in the modern American workplace. Whether you're currently employed and seeking to keep that job or in transition and looking for a new one, it is the only way to achieve your goal. You have to make sure that the expertise you bring to work each day is current, complete and capable of advancing your employer's success. Employ that knowledge on-the-job, and you'll advance your own career, as well.

We Don't Do Careers

We Americans have any number of attributes that uniquely define our culture. That's true in society at large and in the workplace. Normally, these characteristics are healthy and helpful. Sometimes, however, habits that were once benign can suddenly become foolhardy and even harmful. We love our cars, for example, and although many of us have long driven them to work, that easy, comfortable way of doing things now threatens our wallets as well as our environment.

This good-to-bad transformation also applies to our careers. Historically, if you put 100 Americans in a room and asked how many of them set goals for their career and then directed their employment toward the accomplishment of those goals, fewer than ten would raise their hands ... if they were answering the question truthfully. The reality has always been and remains to this day that we don't do careers in the U.S. of A..

You can, of course, put a positive spin on that habit. You could say that we have ignored our careers because we were focused on our employers. Since the 1920s, when President Calvin Coolidge first articulated the notion, most of us have believed that "The business of America is business." What was good for General Motors was good for the USA. And, if we helped make GM or Lehman Brothers or Enron or MCI or any other American employer achieve success, we would be successful too.

No less important, there are only so many hours in the day. Every minute we spend on ourselves is a minute we take away from our employer, so being a loyal, heads-down, hard-at-work employee is simply a part of the way we earn our paycheck. We put our job ahead of our career because we are sure that our employers care about our wellbeing and, therefore, will take care of us, as well.

Now, I'm all for positive thinking, but that view clearly doesn't correlate with our present day reality. In the past, you could treat your career as an afterthought because the world of work just wasn't very dangerous. Stick with that habit today, however, and you'll likely find yourself stuck in place as the world passes you by.

The American workplace is no longer filled with numerous, sturdy career ladders held up by our employers. It has morphed, instead, into a single, huge "career jungle gym" on which there is no prescribed path to success. If you want to have any security at all in this vastly more dynamic and demanding environment, you have to do careers. More specifically, you have to do your own career. If you don't, it will do you.

How Do You Do a Career?

Doing a career means taking charge of your workplace experience. In order to implement such initiative, you have to stop putting your career second. In today's workplace, you and your career must come first.

Why? Because what your employer deserves in return for its paycheck is not a lifetime of loyalty, an 85 hour workweek, or 24/7 connectivity via your Blackberry. While those metrics have, unfortunately, come to be seen as our modern measures of individual commitment, they are not what your employer (or any employer) needs or even wants.

What best serves your employer isn't harder work or more work; it is your best work. And you can't do your best work if your career is weak. To put it another way, you can't take care of your employer unless you take care of yourself – and your career – first. Unless you devote the time and attention required to make your career strong.

What does a strong career look like?

As I explain in my book, *Work Strong: Your Personal Career Fitness System*, a strong career is one with seven attributes. It's a workplace experience where:

- you refresh and expand your expertise in your field of work so that you are always able to perform at the state-of-the-art;

- you extend and nurture your network of contacts in your field and industry so you are always top of mind when opportunities come up;

- you add ancillary skills (e.g., a second language, technological literacy) so you are always extending the contribution you can make with your core expertise;

- you push out the limits of your comfort zone so you are always ready to work in the widest possible range of situations and circumstances;

- you work with those individuals and organizations that will support and advance your career so you are always in an environment where you can succeed;

- you volunteer your talent to community, social service or environmental groups so you always contribute to others' future as well as your own; and

- you pace yourself with appropriate downtime and vacations so you are always rested and ready to perform at your peak on-the-job.

If that sounds like a lot of work, it is – at least in comparison to the effort we expend when we don't do careers. As onerous as such a commitment may seem, however, it begins to make some sense if you remember the Golden Rule.

With a slight modification, that guideline holds all the justification you should need to invest more time and priority in your career. In the treacherous and demanding world of work that is now your present and your future:

> *Do for your career as you would like*
> *your career to do for you.*

Micro Careers

The common view has been that we have one career. Typically, it was defined by both our occupational field – we are an attorney, a salesperson or a logistics professional – and our employer – we are an employee of IBM or Coca- Cola or Geico. Although we were often told otherwise, many of us believed that we would spend our entire career working in that one field and for that one employer. In other words, we were convinced our careers would be relatively stable and long-lasting.

While that was seldom true in the past, it is never true today. The late, unlamented Great Recession has changed the nature of our careers forever. That's an unsettling assertion, I know. But, it's the truth. And, sticking our heads in the sand won't undo what has been done.

On the other hand, if we can learn the new rules – if we can get our arms around them and figure out how to play by and win with them – we can turn today's difficult situation into a much better one tomorrow. We can capture the upside in a down economy. We can put these new rules to work for us so we can find the work we want and hang onto it.

So, what are these new rules? They are a response to the traumatic and wrenching devastation of business now underway in this country and around the world. From GM to Citigroup, from Hertz to Microsoft, employers are shedding jobs and the workers who held them.

These are not, however, your father's or mother's layoffs. They are not reductions-in-force that will eventually be replaced by rehiring-in-force. They are, instead, reductions-in-structure. The American employer is becoming leaner and determined to stay that way.

This shift in organizational philosophy holds several implications for those of us in the workforce.

- *First, there will be far fewer permanent jobs available to us.* Companies will shrink down to a relatively small number of core roles and hire very selectively to fill them. Gone are the days of offering a position to a qualified applicant. Today and for many tomorrows to come, only the person who can excel at a job will get the nod.

- *Second, employers will increase their hiring for "defined outcome positions."* Unlike traditional contract or project work, these situations will have the look and feel of permanent jobs, but have a fixed duration determined by the accomplishment of a specific business objective established by the employer. Defined outcome positions will have the same organizational prestige and seniority as core jobs, but without the commitment to (relatively) long term employment.

- *Third, employers will attempt to be much more nimble and quick acting.* The competitive dynamics of a highly integrated, global marketplace have shortened the life cycle of products and services, sales and marketing strategies, and the organizational staffing requirements that flow from them. The kinds of talent required to execute an organization's business plan last year or the year before may be—indeed, often will be—entirely different than those it needs today or tomorrow.

If those are the new rules, how do we play them?

The answer is as simple as it is challenging. We will have to shift our own employment philosophy. We must change the way we think about our careers. We have to accept that they are no longer relatively stable or long-lasting. From now on, our careers will be episodic and short. They will be "micro careers."

Micro careers are defined by two kinds of impermanence:

- Instead of working for one or two employers over the course of a thirty year career, we will now be employed by 10-12 organizations over the course of a fifty year career. We are living longer even as the staffing needs of employers grow shorter and less enduring.

- Instead of working in a single occupational field, we will work in 3-5 different professions. They will all draw on a common foundation of talent, but each will require a specific and additional set of knowledge, skills and abilities.

This continuous changing means that we can no longer aspire to be complete and fully formed workers. The old industrial era paradigm of moving from novice to journeyman to master is over. In today's knowledge-based economy, only masters survive. So, our new strategy must be to act as "masters-in-progress." We must never stop moving toward a better, more capable, more effective version of our best selves.

Now, I acknowledge that such incessant self-renewal is a new and potentially uncomfortable way of working for some, maybe even many of us. We worked hard to get to a certain point in our careers, and now, we would like to ratchet back our pace and enjoy the fruits of our labor. And, that's no longer possible. In the 21st Century workplace, managing a successful career is like riding a bicycle. We can coast for a short period of time, but we're going to have to peddle and sometimes peddle very hard if we want to keep from crashing.

While that may be difficult to accept, there are some advantages to this situation. It enables us to escape from the imprisonment of dull jobs and dead-end employers. No employment situation is forever, and as long as we keep preparing ourselves for what's ahead, each new job is a chance to move on and up. We get to start fresh on a regular basis, so mistakes are less harmful to our progress and risk is less dangerous. We have, in short, more freedom and opportunity than we have ever had. That's the key point we should remember. Because that's the big benefit of micro careers.

The Vacuum in Our Careers

We're all familiar with bubbles. There was the dot.com bubble in the 1990s and the housing bubble in the early years of this century. They were overheated investments that ultimately fell flat. In our careers, however, we've done exactly the opposite. Most of us have invested little or nothing in our careers, and the resulting vacuum is strangling our future. That sucking sound we hear is our future imploding.

The notion that we could have everything for nothing in our career seems to have emerged with the rise of no-cost content on the Web. Consciously or otherwise, legions of us have come to the conclusion that we can find everything we need to manage our careers success-fully among the free pages posted online. It was inevitable, therefore, that for the first time in modern history, the 2001 recession saw sales of career and job search books actually decline during an economic downturn.

This free lunch investment strategy is undoubtedly alluring, but alas, it's also completely irrational. Think about it. As scary as it may be in today's environment, most of us accept that investing is the only legitimate way to secure and improve our life. We invest to (hope-fully) put money away for retirement. We invest in buying a house with the dream that it will become a home and, eventually, an asset we can leave to our kids. We even invest in gym memberships to improve our physical fitness and in health insurance just in case we need more intensive care.

We make all of those investments, but we act as skinflints when it comes to the one-third of our lives we spend in the workplace. Oh sure, we open our wallets when we first start out. Lots of us invest in getting an education – we pay tuition at a college or trade school – so we have a proper foundation in the world of work. And, while our parents may help us in that endeavor, we recognize and accept the importance of doing so. But after that, we act as if the Bill of Rights guarantees us free job search assistance and career counseling and coaching. In fact, asking a person in transition to invest in his or her career is often viewed as a vile effort to take advantage of them.

And tragically, nothing could be further from the truth. Indeed, not asking us to invest in ourselves and our future is a startling denial of our own capacity to succeed. Setting us apart as some sort of protected class, while well meaning, inevitably has two perverse impacts:

- It creates a dependency that subliminally signals to each and every one of us that we don't have what it takes to mend our own situation and take care of ourselves;

and

- It establishes a sense of entitlement that actually handicaps us and prevents us from taking the necessary action to help ourselves.

Setting Us Up for Even Harder Times

Equally as important, when we're told that we need not invest in ourselves in tough times, many of us conclude that the same is true in good times, as well. That perspective, more than any other, is probably what's behind the deteriorating skills and knowledge many of us bring to work each day.

We're falling behind the rest of the world in research, productivity and value creation because the conventional wisdom is that it's not our job to keep up. Whether we're a Boomer, GenY or a Millennial, we've been taught that we bear no personal responsibility for staying at the state-of-the-art in our field or for acquiring the expertise to manage our own career.

The most telling evidence of this situation can be found at a local "job club." Every meeting, these days, attracts hundreds of well educated, middle-aged professionals who have never before been unemployed. Now that they are, however, they lack the tools to get reemployed. They worked hard at their jobs, they were loyal to their employers, but neither of those attributes protected them from a pink slip and neither can put them back to work.

The structure and dynamic of the workplace has changed, and they haven't. They were misled by the free lunch crowd, so they haven't invested in acquiring the skills and knowledge of career self-management. And, without that expertise, they are unable to protect themselves from today's disruptive economy. For them, the sucking sound is almost deafening.

But, it doesn't have to stay that way. It is possible to turn our fortunes around. The solution is admittedly easy to offer and more difficult to implement. It has the merit, however, of being absolutely right for the times. The key to survival and prosperity in the 21st Century world of work is continuous *self-investment*.

If you're in transition, go back to school in your field even as you look for a new opportunity. If you're lucky enough to be employed, get some training that will add to your ability to contribute on-the-job. And regardless of your situation, make sure that you get smarter about how best to manage your own career. Such investments will never produce a bubble; they will, in contrast, quiet the deafening din by filling the vacuum with opportunity.

Swimming With Something On

Warren Buffet described the impact of the current financial turmoil in the American economy this way: "You only learn who's been swimming naked when the tide goes out." It's a wonderfully instructive image. A high tide covers a lot of missteps and oversights, while a low tide makes them visible for all to see. Witness the emperors on Wall Street who are now running around without their designer (or any other) apparel.

The same is true with your career. When times are good, when the economy is firing on all pistons and employers are hungry for new hires, you can get away with a lot of weak spots on your occupational balance sheet. When the economy goes south, however, when employers suddenly get much pickier about who they hire and, no less important, who they retain, those aneurysms can lead to career cardiac arrest or what most of us call unemployment.

What Should You Do?

How do you protect yourself in today's lowest of low tides economy? Make sure you're swimming with something on, something that will protect you from the environment and enable you to glide more powerfully through the waters ahead. To pull it off, however, you'll need a new outlook and a different way of training.

A New Outlook

To be a strong swimmer in the white water workplace of the 21st Century, you have to build a healthy career first. You have to develop and maintain career fitness. Why? Because your goal has changed. You're not trying to achieve job security – there is no such thing in the ever-changing workplace of the 21st Century – you're pushing through the turbulence to reach genuine and lasting "career security."

Job security is something an employer controls and calibrates according to its financial health. We all know how it works: when times are good, you've got a job; when times are bad, the job disappears and so must you. In short, job security never has and never will have anything at all to do with you. It is all about the security of the job, and from an employer's perspective, jobs are simply boxes on an org chart. You can add them, move them around or erase them at will. The workers involved are simply collateral damage.

Career security, in contrast, is something you control, and it depends entirely on the health of your career. Career security describes your ability to find employment consistently and always in a job and with an organization that will enable you to express and experience your natural (and best) talent. It isn't a matter of settling for the first available job or employer, but rather seeking out and successfully landing the right job with the right employer for you. Career security, then, is your capacity to act as a "smart consumer" of both employment opportunities and organizational employers at each and every stage in your career.

A Different Way of Training

Achieving career security doesn't happen by magic or wishful thinking. It isn't some inalienable right granted to you by the Constitution or deeded to you by the status of your family or guaranteed to you by the pedigree of the school you attended. No, being secure in your career comes only from developing a vital capacity for superior work. It is the measure of the effort you make to ensure your access to the American

Dream.

How do you build and maintain career security? You commit yourself to a regimen of employment-strengthening activities that you practice on a regular basis. The five steps in the process will stretch you a bit, at least at first, and like anything else that's important, they do require an investment of time and effort on your part. The return on that effort, however, is both unique and singularly important. The Career Fitness Regimen will empower you to increase both the paycheck and the satisfaction you bring home from work.

Here's how it works:

Step 1: Learn the principles involved in managing your career so that you do what's best for you and do it consistently.

Step 2: Identify your natural talent – your inherent capacity for excellence and the only foundation on which you can build a meaningful and rewarding career.

Step 3: Set near and longer term career goals as well as a developmental goal that will enable you to progress from one to the other.

Step 4: Learn and then apply the practices that will increase the strength, reach and endurance of your career (see Micro Careers for more detail).

Step 5: Record and regularly review your status so you can recognize and celebrate your progress and identify and remediate your shortcomings.

Collectively, those steps enable you to understand what's involved in career self-management and how to execute it successfully. They are the pillars of the "system" for building Career Fitness that I introduced in my book, *Work Strong: Your Personal Career Fitness System*. Think of it as a plan for preserving and protecting your part in the American Dream.

Now, I know what you're thinking – the tide is already out, so isn't such an effort way too late? Aren't some of us – maybe many of us – already exposed and therefore swimming at the mercy of the elements?

Yes and no. If you find that you've been working without protective cover, the next year or two will probably be a rough slog. However, your situation is not permanent or irreparable. Start now to insulate your career. Commit yourself to the Career Fitness Regimen. Because the tide will come back in, and when it does, you'll be prepared. You'll have the resilience to cut through the water no matter how choppy it gets. You'll have career security.

You Gotta Work Strong to Work

Ask almost anyone in the workplace today, and they will tell you they are doing a good job. While they might acknowledge that their work isn't perfect, they take pride in what they do and the contribution they believe they are making to their employer. So, how come one-sixth of the workforce has been hit with what seems like a layoff out-of-the-blue? What's behind the pink slip so many of us never saw coming? The answer lies in the changing definition of security.

Historically, the key to security has been dedication, loyalty and most importantly, hard work on-the-job. If you gave your employer your all, it would repay you with all of the work you needed.

Millions of Americans are still convinced that the best way to protect themselves in this stuttering economy is with long hours and never-ending devotion to their job. Just look at all of the frenetic checking of office email that now goes on while people are at home in the evening, on vacation with their family and in their doctor's waiting room when they're sick.

Of course, we would like to believe that this effort will pay off in employment security, but the evidence is overwhelming that it doesn't. Over 16 million Americans have discovered that working hard won't save them from a pink slip.

Is there something that will? Absolutely. In today's world of work, you gotta' work strong to work.

How do you do that? You have to change both your focus and your priority. You have to shift your focus from your job to your career. And you have to shift your priority from what you do for your employer to what you do for yourself. Here's what I mean.

Change Your Focus

When you focus on your job, you serve the interests of your employer. That's not a bad thing, but in practice, it crowds everything else out. Think about it. When you're devoted to your job – when you're concentrating on doing everything you must and everything you can to accomplish everything that's been assigned to you – there simply isn't any time left over for you. The benefits of working hard are a one-way street. They all accrue to your employer.

It wasn't always that way, of course. In the past, accepting work that exclusively benefited your employer was counterbalanced by a job security you could (theoretically) count on. Today, it isn't. As we've all learned the hard way, the economy is just too unstable for employers to deliver on such a guarantee, even if they promise it.

So, what's the alternative? Focus on your career. Concentrate on building up the capability, flexibility, utility and visibility of your talent— your DNA of excellence.

Become so good in your area of expertise and so generous with the contribution you make with it that there are always employers looking for you. When you put yourself in that position, you are assured of continuous employment in your choice of jobs. That's called "career security," and it's the only kind of protection you can count on in today's world of work.

Change Your Priority

Traditionally (and legally), employment has been defined as an "at will" experience. To put it bluntly, you serve at the will of your employers. You get a job only if they offer one, and you work only as long as they will employ you. Humans may be creatures with free will, but in the 20th Century workplace, only employers got to exercise it.

Happily, that concept has now been overtaken by events. Today, employers are desperate to find and hire talented workers. They even describe their situation as a "War for Talent." In the face of record unemployment, they believe there is a critical shortage of two kinds of people: those who have certain rare talents (e.g., nursing, engineering, IT) and those who use their talent to excel on-the-job.

What does that mean for you? If you can position yourself as a person with one or both of those attributes, you will reverse the definition of "at will." You will be able to take a job only if you want to and you will be able to work only where you have a genuine opportunity to succeed.

That's called working smart. When you do so, you change the nature of your employment experience. Your career is no longer a one-way street where all of the benefit accrues to your employer. It is, instead, a more equitable two-way street where you benefit as much as the organization. In effect, you create your own security – the only security worth having.

The Career Activist Republic

The common understanding of talent limits it to exceptional people who engage in exceptional activities. According to this view, only a very few individuals have talent, and their talent is expressed in only the most rarified of fields and feats. The rest of us are out of luck.

People of talent are professional athletes, entertainers and artists. An opera singer at the Metropolitan Opera in New York City has talent while the best a bank teller or a plumber can be is good at their job. Talent, Americans are taught and told, isn't something the masses have nor is it really talented to be an exceptional performer in unexceptional occupations.

The Conventional Elitism of Talent

Ascribing talent to only a select few is a pretension that strikes at the very heart of human equality and the American democracy. This elitism of talent has its roots in the industrial era. In the early decades of the 20th Century, mass manufacturers—most notably those that produced cars and food—needed workers who would labor like machines or beast of burden and perform the same tasks over and over again.

Happy to respond, the social arbiters of the time created the conceit of America's "unwashed masses." This notion set common people – the working class – apart from their more educated and cultured betters. It was a derogatory description which created two distinct groups: those with brains and everybody else.

Not to be outdone, the country's academic establishment reinforced the talent divide by introducing a developmental structure and programmatic format designed to relegate all but an exceptional few to mediocrity. Called "gifted and talented" programs in elementary school and "advanced placement" in high school, these initiatives didn't just serve the needs of smart kids – an admirable goal. They also communicated a sense of inferiority to all those who were not selected. In effect, the "normal" kids were told they didn't have talent or advanced capabilities and thus were second class citizens in the nation's educational system.

The Duke University Talent Identification Program, for example, describes itself as "a global leader in identifying academically gifted students and providing them with innovative programming to support their development." In other words, a person isn't talented unless they are academically gifted. If a child doesn't score high on some so-called "intelligence test," they aren't smart enough to do extraordinary things in life and thus should receive only uncreative programming and support.

A More Pluralistic Perspective

The dictionary, thankfully, takes a more pluralistic view of talent. It defines the word as "the natural endowments of a person" and an endowment as "a natural gift, ability or quality." There is no qualifier limiting talent to extraordinary people or to extraordinary endeavors. The term is not reserved for the infallible and famous or even for the in-your-face and infamous. Quite the contrary, talent is a natural characteristic of the human species and is expressed in the full range of its idiosyncratic interests and occupations.

There is talent in being an exceptional salesperson and an extraordinary truck driver. Talent can be expressed by an especially good customer service representative and bank teller, and by a truly outstanding electrician, mechanic, carpenter and computer programmer. The talent is not in what a person does, but in how they do it. Talent, then, is the expression of excellence, and that excellence can be attained in any and every profession, craft and trade.

In addition, the contempt with which many traditional talent elites are now held among the general public has further undermined their claim to specialness. Thanks to athletes who use steroids to set records, entertainers who indulge in sophomoric behavior to make headlines, business and investment gurus who commit criminal acts to enrich themselves, and politicians who can't seem to act at all despite the pressing issues of our day, people simply no longer believe that those who have traditionally been viewed as being talented are also extraordinary beings. Despite the nation's tabloid fascination with them, most Americans have concluded that talent elites are no better and often much worse than everybody else. And since that's so, the rest of the population is just as likely to have talent as the so-called superstars are.

This shift in perspective recasts talent as a trait that:

- all people possess, regardless of their social standing, fame or fortune;

and

- each and every individual can use to be accomplished in their life's work.

These two principles undergird the democratization of talent. They form the foundation for a new movement in the American workplace. Called the Career Activist Republic, this emerging culture affirms the nobility of all human work and of all of those who perform it. It recognizes that, despite the differences among Americans in their ethnicity, gender and national origin, they are all equal persons of talent. Each and every one of them.

What You Need to Know Next: Career Success Tactics That Actually Work in the New Workplace

NOTES

UnNatural Work Sells You Short

For many people, work is an onerous, often frustrating and even demeaning experience. It is something they do in order to enjoy the rest of their life. If you find that hard to believe, consider this: according to research, an astonishing 88% of all Americans daydream at work about quitting their job to do something else.

Why are so many people so unhappy with their employment?

They are doing unNatural work. They have an inherent talent – every human being does – but they find themselves employed in a career that ignores or, worse, tramples on that capability.

I call this talent your Natural because it is as integral a part of who you are as your personality. It is an essential element of your individual definition. Of what makes you a unique and special person.

Your Natural is something you love to do and do well. The doing of it comes naturally to you – it is a ready-made talent – and excelling at it gives you an extraordinary sense of satisfaction – a feeling of fulfillment.

Your Natural is not a position title or an occupation. You do not work at your Natural as a senior project manager or a doctor, a lawyer or an Indian chief. You do so by engaging in an activity that is central to success in the performance of those roles.

For example, Lance Armstrong is a champion cyclist. His Natural, however, is not professional cycling. It is his talent for agility, endurance and stamina. He chose to apply his Natural to the sport of cycling, but he could have been just as successful and just as fulfilled in another occupation if excellence in that occupation depended on agility, endurance and stamina – his natural talent.

What does that mean for the rest of us in the world of work?

First, we are all super stars-in-waiting.

Every single one of us has a Lance Armstrong, a Susan Boyle, a Sully Sullenberger inside us. We can realize that champion in our career – we can express and experience our ready-made talent on-the-job – but only if we are working in an occupation that requires our Natural to be successful.

Second, using our Natural is a key element of what makes us a unique person.

The Human Genome Project proved that, as different as we may seem on the outside, we are only 3 percent different on the inside. Putting our Natural to work is one of the ways we achieve that 3 percent and establish ourselves as distinguishable and distinguished individuals.

Third, our Natural is a raw talent that needs nurturing.

It's up to us to discover it and then to refine it. We must continuously stretch its capacity and our ability to apply it in our work. Captain Sullenberger didn't perform a heroic feat of flying by simply climbing in the cockpit each day and going through the motions. He practiced regularly and rigorously to build up his ability to use his Natural to its fullest, and he needed every bit of that skill to land his place safely and achieve the "miracle on the Hudson."

Fourth, when we ignore our Natural at work, we waste our shot at becoming the person of our dreams.

Almost nine-out-of-ten Americans can imagine the superstar inside them, but for one reason or another, they fail to bring that person to work with them. Yet, it's our work, more than any other human endeavor, that provides the kind of challenges that draw out the best we can be. It alone gives us a chance to experience the champion inside us.

And when we fail to take advantage of that opportunity – when we accept employment in an occupation or a job that does not put our Natural to work – it feels toxic. Because it is. Doing unNatural work prevents us from performing at our peak, and the resulting substandard performance harms us in two ways:

- *It jeopardizes our employment.* Doing anything less than our best work in today's demanding workplace is a guaranteed seat on the fast train to early termination.

- *It undercuts our happiness.* It prevents us from feeling the profound sense of satisfaction that comes from knowing we have been tested in a fair way – one that challenges the best of ourselves – and measured up.

You will spend one-third or more of your life on-the-job. Don't sell that time short. Fill it with work that comes naturally to you so you can express and experience your personal champion.

Take Your Talent to Work Day

You are destined to be nothing special, so you might as well accept it. That was the message from a prominent career counselor writing in a major news magazine in 2010. As he blithely put it, "Failures may help you realize you are average; not everyone can be a star." And then, just to smack you down a little further, he adds the following obtusely patronizing observation: "But plain folk are worthy too." Thanks for the reassurance, pal.

This view that a special few of us are the chosen ones and everyone else is a dim wit is so 20th Century. It's the career analogue to the hubristic self-indulgence that brought us the Great Recession. For years, the sycophants of business school capitalism crowed that the wizards of Wall Street and the CEOs of corporate America were so much smarter than the rest of us ordinary folk ... only now, we know they weren't (and aren't). They were the Masters of Stupidity, which is a talent, I suppose, but not one that makes you a star.

If there is a silver lining to this terrible economic time, it is the dawning realization that those who were supposedly our "betters" actually aren't. That doesn't mean, however, that we should be satisfied with mediocrity. Bringing down the so-called elite a peg or two doesn't mean that we can't or shouldn't move ourselves up an equal distance or more. Despite what that career pundit would have you believe, you are not the prisoner of some drab average existence ... unless you permit yourself to be.

You and every other person on this planet have an extraordinary being living inside you, waiting for a chance to perform. If you don't believe that, think about Susan Boyle. She was a less than attractive Scottish spinster until she strode out on the stage of a British television show and wowed the world with her voice. That talent has always been there, but she had never had the courage or the opportunity to express it.

And sadly, that experience is the way many of us live our careers, only unlike Susan Boyle, we retire without giving our special talent a stage. We leave it unrecognized and unused because we lack either the self-confidence or the opportunity to expose it to the light of day.

- We don't think our talent is worthy enough for others – especially our family and friends – to respect it as a career.

- Or, we don't see our talent as valuable enough to be a career because it won't enable us to keep up with the Madoffs.

- Or, worse, we buy into the nonsense of that condescending career counselor and accept the notion that we are simply beasts of burden with a vocabulary – average beings in heels and loafers.

So, What Should You Do?

I urge you to participate in a new workplace event. You've undoubtedly heard of Take Your Child to Work Day and its analog for those without children, Take Your Pet to Work Day. Well, I propose that you indulge yourself in a similarly special activity. I call it *Take Your Talent to Work Day*.

Take Your Talent to Work Day is an event open to you and everyone else. Here's how it works.

> *First (and this is the hardest part), give yourself permission to take the time and make the effort to solve one of the great mysteries of life: what is it that you particularly enjoy doing and do particularly well.*

I call it your Natural, because it is a gift that comes naturally to you. We all have such a talent but many, maybe even most of us hide, it away in a hobby or passion we pursue outside of work. Ironically, however, when we use our Natural, we unlock the handcuffs of drab work that makes us average. We unleash the world class performer – the Susan Boyle – who lives within every single one of us.

> *Second (and this is only a little less hard), give yourself permission to explore all of the possibilities so you can make one of the great discoveries of life: which occupation will enable you to put your special talent to work on-the-job.*

The key to success in such a search is to put aside self-imposed constraints (e.g., I can't make enough money doing it) and the biases, however well meaning, of friends and family (e.g., You have so much more to give than that.). You have an inalienable right to pursue happiness at work. That is the essence of the American Dream and, no less important, it's a form of compensation that is every bit as valuable as the money you earn.

You spend most of your adult life at work, so shouldn't that time be as rewarding an experience as the time you spend outside the workplace? Of course, it should. So, show yourself what you can do: Take Your Talent to Work today, tomorrow and for the rest of your career.

The Alpha Career Athlete

We've all heard of the alpha male and female. The dictionary defines them as the dominant person in a group, the one everybody emulates and follows. The term was originally coined to describe behavior in wolf and dog packs, but for most of the 20th Century, it also accurately depicted the way we interacted in our careers. One person was on top, and the rest of us brought up the rear.

While wolves and dogs are stuck with this leader-follower relationship, however, we humans have an option. We can pull ourselves out of the back of the pack – out of the pack altogether, in fact – and assume a new role. I call it the "alpha career athlete." It recognizes our innate ability to act as individuals and to set our own unique course in the world of work.

More often than not, the alpha career athlete still finds their employment in an organization. Most aren't free agents or independent contractors. They work in teams, on projects and for departments, and they report to a boss. Their on-the-job experience is similar to that of every other person in the workplace. What changes is their view of who they are working for and why.

An alpha career athlete works on themselves for themselves. They are interested in learning just how good they can be in their profession, craft or trade. They accept a job because it challenges them to be better than they have been, and they devote all of their talent to passing the test. Moreover, that same commitment to self-improvement also enhances the value of their contribution to their employer. In effect, they protect their employment and preserve their paycheck by persevering in their determination to excel.

In Search of (Personal) Excellence

In 1982, Tom Peters wrote a business classic called *In Search of Excellence.* The book's popularity was largely based on the author's research into how companies achieved superior performance. It outlined a number of practices that other organizations could implement in order to achieve their own version of excellence.

What many readers missed, however, was the underlying premise of the book: success was best achieved through a commitment to excellence. If you wanted your company to prosper, it wasn't enough to be good or even very good and certainly not mediocre or just good enough to get by. The one sure pathway to prosperity was excellence.

What was true for organizations in the 20th Century is true for individuals in the 21st Century. Success is not achieved by being loyal to one's employer or by knowing how things get done inside an organization. It is not assured with years of experience or even with a knowledge of the current state-of-the-art. What produces sustained career advancement in today's world of work is a commitment to personal excellence.

It is what drives the alpha career athlete. He or she is "in search of excellence." They are on a quest to become the champion inside them. This is not some quixotic adventure, but rather an entirely rational determination to express and experience the talent with which they (and all of us) were created. Alpha career athletes believe that, just as every company can achieve superior performance, so too can they. And they're resolved to do so.

Companies, however, have Peters' guidelines with which to work; alpha career athletes need something else. They need a set of practices that will engage, refine and unleash the excellence within them. What follows are what I think those practices must be:

I. Pump Up Your Cardiovascular System.
The heart of your career is your occupational expertise. Re-imagine yourself as a work-in-progress so that you are always adding depth and tone to your knowledge and skill set.

II. Strengthen Your Circulatory System.
The wider and deeper your network of contacts, the more visible you and your capabilities will be in the workplace. Make nurturing professional relationships a part of your business day.

III. Develop All of Your Muscle Groups.
The greater your versatility in contributing your expertise at work, the broader the array of situations and assignments in which you can be employed. Develop ancillary skills that will give you more ways to apply your core expertise in the workplace.

IV. Increase Your Flexibility & Range of Motion.
Moving from industry-to-industry, from one daily schedule to another or even from one location to another is never easy, but your willingness to adapt will help to keep your career moving forward.

V. Work With Winners.
Working with successful organizations and coworkers enables you to grow on-the-job, develop useful connections that will last a career and establish yourself as a winner in the world of work.

VI. Stretch Your Soul.
A healthy career not only serves you, it serves others, as well. A personal commitment to doing some of your best work as good works for your community, your country and/or our planet is the most invigorating form of work/life balance.

VII. Pace Yourself.
A fulfilling and rewarding career depends upon your getting the rest and replenishment you need in order to do your best work every day you're on-the-job. Discipline yourself and your boss to set aside time to recharge your passion and capacity for work.

All of us have the inherent ability to be an alpha career athlete because all of us have an inherent talent that wants to be – deserves to be – discovered. Humans are the only beings, however, who can willfully choose to ignore their gift. And happily, they are also the only beings who can choose to recognize it. So, become the alpha career athlete you were meant to be; put yourself in search of (personal) excellence.

Career Victories

Back in the day, accomplishments at work were only accomplishments if they were acknowledged by a supervisor. That reality had at least two downsides for you. First, it limited the definition of an accomplishment to whatever made sense to your supervisor, whether or not it made any sense at all for you. And second, your accomplishments were only recognized if your supervisor bothered to do so, and sadly, not all supervisors have good human relations skills.

The net effect of this situation was to diminish your perception of your accomplishments. If you have any doubt about that, think back to the last time you wrote a resume. Remember how hard it was to recall your achievements in your most recent job, let alone those in jobs you held earlier in your career? That fuzziness indicates how little impact your accomplishments have had on your own sense of success at work.

Such a malformed view of your role at work is a threat to you and to your career. It undermines your self-image and, ultimately, your self-confidence in your own capability. Equally as ominous, it clouds how people see your contribution on-the-job and potential in the workplace. If you are only as accomplished as your supervisor acknowledges, they are in control of what happens to you and your career, and nothing could be more dangerous in today's ultra- demanding world of work.

What should you do about this situation?

Throw out supervisor-defined accomplishments and focus, instead, on personal "career victories." A career victory is different from an old fashioned accomplishment in several ways:

- *First, a career victory is defined by you.* You set a goal – I will improve my work skills or I will increase my output on-the-job – and you determine what constitutes reaching that goal – I will improve my work skills by completing this course of instruction or I will increase my output on-the-job by learning how to use that software program.

- *Second, career victories occur wherever you say they do.* They may happen on-the-job or outside it, in an academic institution, a professional association or a volunteer activity. A career victory is not limited to what happens in your employer's workplace; it describes what happens to you – the self-improvements you realize by reaching goals you set – in whatever venue you select.

- *Third, career victories occur however you say they do.* They are not dictated by what best serves your supervisor or employer. A career victory may certainly do that, but its purpose is to reinforce your self-esteem and advance your career. You decide what self-improvement will do you the most good and the conditions under which it will be realized.

- *Fourth, career victories occur whenever you say they do.* They don't depend upon your supervisor's ability to recognize them or their willingness to express that recognition in a way that will do you any good. A career victory is a success that you recognize, and it is a well deserved pat on the back that you give yourself.

Career victories are based on a very simple, but powerful premise. It analogizes achieving career success to riding a bicycle. In other words, you can coast for a short while in your career, but most of the time, you're going to have to peddle – you're going to have to engage in continuous self-improvement – to keep making steady progress. If you don't, your career will start to wobble and eventually topple over.

Although this concept may seem a bit strange at first, it's not all that hard to get used to. After all, almost all of us know how to ride a bike. And even if we haven't done so for awhile, it's one of those skills you never really lose and thus can quickly regain. Achieving career victories, therefore, is something anybody and everybody can do. They are a democratic activity. And, unlike accomplishments, where recognition can be colored by the biases and limitations of your supervisor, they are an equal opportunity form of celebration.

You can use your career victories in several ways. To start, I suggest that you memorialize your victories in writing by creating a "career record" – a diary of sorts that describes all of your work-related successes. This document isn't a resume, although it can certainly make writing a resume much easier. It is, instead, a simple listing of your self-improvement goals and what you did to meet them. That record, in turn, can help you see your progress in the world of work so you can celebrate your successes (whether or not they are recognized by your employer's performance appraisal system). And, it can provide a wake-up call if you find yourself coasting along and losing momentum in your career.

Focusing on your career victories doesn't mean that your contributions on-the-job are any less important. Indeed, they can and should be career victories to which you aspire and for which you strive. The reason you do so, however, is not to gain the recognition of your supervisor, but instead to express and experience the best you can be. That's the true definition of success in the modern workplace.

An Investment of Caring

There's a view these days that successful online networking is based on a very simple mathematical formula. A lot of contacts equals a lot of employment opportunities. If that were so, however, all of those people who are now feverishly connecting, friending and following would feel more secure in their jobs and more confident about their careers. Networking is important in achieving success, but what many people are doing today is "notworking" and, as a consequence, wasting their time.

Networking is one of those rare words that says exactly what it means. It's netWORK. To be effective:

- you have to make networking an integral part of your work day. It is something you should do when you're satisfied with your current employment and when you're looking to move to a better opportunity.

- you have to work hard at your networking. You must devote a sufficient amount of time and genuine effort to the activity and you have to stick with it, even when it feels like way too much work.

Think of it as an investment you make in your future, but one that will only pay off if you do it right.

Why bother? Because one-third of all open jobs are never advertised. They're filled by networking – by one person knowing another person who puts them in touch with a third who lands the job. That time-tested process is the single best way to capture a promotion or more interesting role. It ensures you're top of mind with referrers and decision-makers and helps to validate your credentials during evaluation and selection.

So, what's the key to successful networking? You have to understand exactly what kind of investment works best. Contrary to conventional thinking, it's not the quantity but the quality of the activity that matters.

You see, networking is not a contact sport. The goal is not to score a lot of connections, friends and followers. An ever-widening circle of acquaintances is important, but it will do you little good if those contacts are virtually unknown to you and you to them.

Your mother told you never to speak to strangers. She would have been equally as wise to advise you never to let a contact remain a stranger. Make new acquaintances, but do so to build a relationship with them. Said another way, networking is most effective when you see it as your opportunity to make an investment of caring – to show others that you are as interested in them as you hope they will be in you.

An Investment That Works

A meaningful relationship – especially one that will largely or even entirely exist on the Web – depends upon two critical factors: familiarity and trust. The people with whom you interact must feel as if they know you and that they can count on you to have their best interests at heart.

How can you establish those factors without the body language and tone of voice we rely on in the real world? How can you convince people that you truly care about them when all or most of your communications will occur online?

You have to communicate with a theme. Every message you send must convey one simple, but powerful idea. It must resonate with: *I thought of you.*

You can impart that theme in two ways:

- In general messages, that pass along information which everyone in your network is likely to find interesting, newsworthy or, most importantly, helpful (as they look for a new job or strive to advance their career).

and

- In targeted messages, that pass along information which a specific individual in your network is likely to find gracious, kind or helpful (by remembering their birthday or alerting them to an advancement opportunity in which they might be interested).

In both cases, you are taking the time and making the effort to help others. You are, in fact, thinking of them. Your investment in caring is denominated in generosity and compassion. Those attributes provide their own reward, of course, but more often than not they lead to an additional return on your investment. They earn you the interest and support of others, and in today's tough economic climate, nothing is more valuable.

Career Security

A recent poll of U.S. workers found that the one thing we most want from our employers is job security. While that's completely understandable in today's crazy world of work, I'm afraid we're more likely to get a visit from our fairy godmother.

The global economy is now more interconnected and interdependent than at any other time in history. If government economic policies change in China, U.S. producers are affected. If consumer tastes change in Europe, American businesses feel the impact. If a South American company goes bankrupt, the people working in its plant in Tennessee will be hurt.

It is a highly turbulent and unpredictable environment. And that uncertainty makes it all but impossible for our employers – whether they are American or foreign-based organizations – to predict what kinds of talent they will need tomorrow or the day after, let alone six months from now. As a result, they might promise us job security, but they can't deliver it.

If you don't believe me, consider this. The average tenure of a CEO in their job is now down to less than four years. If that insecurity can happen in the corner office, it can (and will) happen everywhere else in the organization.

But, you know what? I'm delighted that job security has joined the gold watch and buggy whip. Think about it. Job security was something only employers could provide, and they did so only when it suited their financial interests. We had no control over the situation, so we stood around hat-in-hand, hoping for a little something we could count on from organizations that were more interested in counting their profits.

What's the alternative? *Career security.*

Career security is the ability to stay employed in jobs of our choosing, regardless of the economic situation in any country or the financial condition of any one employer. Career security is something we create for ourselves, so we control what happens to us in the workplace. We become the master of our career, rather than its victim.

Instead of hoping that our employer will hang onto us when its business turns down, we monitor the employer's status and if it starts to weaken, we take the initiative and move to a new workplace opportunity. Instead of wishing upon a star when our employer gets bought, moved to a new location or reorganized, we line up options with other organizations to ensure our star keeps rising.

Now, some employers will say that such behavior is disloyal. It's not. There are always two parties in the expression of loyalty, and loyalty only makes sense when there's reciprocity between them. In other words, if we are loyal to our employers, they should offer their loyalty to us in return. The death of job security, however, has destroyed that reciprocity. Employers can no longer be loyal to us, so we must be loyal to ourselves. And, career security is the way we do so.

How is Career Security Achieved?

Achieving career security involves three steps:

- *First, we have to get to know ourselves.* We have to figure out what we love to do and do best. That's not our passion; it's our talent. Everyone is born with a natural capability or talent, but only those who take care of it – those who never stop developing its range and depth – can achieve career security. And to make such a commitment, we have to know what our talent is.

- *Second, we have to take our talent to work.* We have to arrive with all of our talent each day and use it to do our best work every day. Employers are desperate for such high performing employees. In fact, according to the Society for Human Resource Management, 70% are now paying bonuses to hire talented contributors, and 65% are paying above market salaries to hang onto them.

- *Third, we must keep our career strong.* We can only work at our talent and use it to do our best work if we are employed by the right organizations and in the right jobs. Career self-management by hoping for the best (or waiting for our employers to deliver it) is a sure-fire formula for career cardiac arrest or what most of us call unemployment. Proactively reaching for opportunities where we can excel, in contrast, is the single best way to increase both the paycheck and the satisfaction we bring home from work.

Job security is definitely an attractive idea, but it's an idea whose time has passed. Career security, on the other hand, is a concept fit for the turbulent world of work in the 21st Century. It has the power and the promise to position us for enduring success. And, it is acquired from the only source we can really count on – ourselves.

A Career Do-Over

One of John Lennon's most famous songs is entitled *Just Like Starting Over*. It's a love poem, but I think it holds a powerful lesson for many of us in the world of work, as well. The song begins with the soft ringing of a bell and then Lennon makes this simple declaration: "We have grown. We have grown."

It's a wonderful way to look at what is often viewed as a setback in our careers. Having to start over seems to imply that we have wasted everything that has gone before. The lessons we have learned, the character we have developed, the wisdom we have gained are somehow diminished because our careers have taken a new tack. That's especially true if the departure is sudden and unexpected as has been the case for so many Americans recently.

Now, I'm very respectful of how upsetting such situations can be. Most of us don't like change, and nobody likes change that is forced on them. That said, I don't think that starting over is all that bad IF we remember that "We have grown. We have grown."

That fact of life doesn't diminish the negative side of starting over, but it does add a strong positive side to the experience. In fact, I think anyone with any time at all in the workplace would be well served to see such a transition as a "career do-over" – a chance to tap into four genuine advantages that come from having grown even just a bit.

What are those four advantages? Here's my list:

Advantage #1: You're smarter than you were.

Being forced to start over means that you get to pick a career field, a specialty or a new employer using all of the insight and knowledge you've gained in the past. Unlike your first career decisions – which were probably made when you were all of 20 or 21 – you actually know something about how the world works. You're a little older and, hopefully, a lot wiser. Your choice, therefore, is apt to be more rationally determined and better suited to what you can do and do best.

Advantage #2: You get to put your mistakes behind you.

You've undoubtedly made mistakes along the way in your career – as we see on the evening news every night, even the most successful among us make errors in judgment – and those mistakes can degrade your career opportunities and momentum. Being forced to start over wipes the slate clean and gives you a chance to embark on a new direction without all of that baggage. Basically, you get to learn from your miscalculations without having to deal with the consequences.

Advantage #3: You are able to reach for what was once unreachable.

Lots of us get into ruts – occupations or roles that no longer interest or challenge us as they once did – but more often than not, we just put our heads down and press on. Our responsibilities and needs trump our innate inclination to correct a situation or improve our lot. Being forced to start over, however, removes those (self-imposed) constraints. You now have the freedom to re-image yourself in a new and more interesting career field, industry or employer, and that liberates you to set new goals and reach for new stars.

Advantage #4: You get to prove yourself to yourself.

Being forced to start over is often confused with failure. That's a backwards way of looking at the situation, for if you look at it from any other perspective, what you'll see is a new beginning. A precious opportunity to prove to yourself that you still have what it takes to succeed.

Picking yourself up and pushing on makes a powerful statement about your character. It demonstrates, beyond any doubt, that you have the right stuff – the courage and determination to survive and, better than that, prosper in even the toughest of times.

Almost nobody likes to start over, but doing so need not be a horrible and demeaning experience. In fact, it can be a profoundly positive turn of events, especially if we remember the wise words of John Lennon. "We have grown. We have grown." And that growth gives us an enormous edge; it gives us resilience and hope.

The Weak Link Syndrome

It was partly my own fault. I realize that now. I naively accepted an invitation on LinkedIn to connect with someone I didn't know. I did confirm that this person was in the employment field, and since I'm terrible at remembering names, I thought that we may have met at a conference somewhere. I still don't know whether that's the case, but as soon as I accepted the invitation, this person started to spam me with email after email about openings he was trying to fill. And therein lies the central problem with LinkedIn, at least as it is currently used by a very large number of people.

LinkedIn advertises itself as a networking tool for professionals. That's fine. But building up a huge (or even a small) address book of contacts is not networking. In fact, given that networking is actually a form of dialogue that is most appropriately practiced as an integral part of one's business day, what's going on at LinkedIn today is best described as "notworking."

You see, the Golden Rule of Networking is that you have to give as good as you get. It's fundamentally an exchange of information, ideas, and/or assistance from which <u>both</u> parties derive value. That mutual allocation of benefit establishes familiarity and trust, and those two factors are the twin pillars of a relationship. When networking is working, that's what it creates – a relationship.

How Do Relationships Happen?

Now, if you've ever been in a relationship, you know two things about them. First, you quickly learn that they are hard work. That's why the word is spelled the way it is: it's netWORK, not net-get-around-to-it-whenever-you-feel-like-it. And second, you come to appreciate that relationships take time to develop. They don't happen with the click of a mouse, whether you're on LinkedIn or Facebook or any other social or professional "networking" site.

And sadly, my connection on LinkedIn understood neither of those points. As he put it when I asked him to stop sending me his intrusive email, "When you linked to me you agreed to receive email notifications and to network with me."

Well, my friend, that's not networking. First, you're not working at building a relationship with me. You're spamming me with unwanted email. Second, there's no reciprocity here. All of the value in our interaction accrues to you. You want me to provide the names of people I know for your openings, yet you haven't taken the time to get to know me or to offer me anything of commensurate value. You aren't giving as good as you get. You're just taking what's useful to you.

Now, I've heard the stories about people finding a job through their LinkedIn contacts. That's great. But those situations are the exception to the rule. There are more than 100 million people with profiles on LinkedIn, and most have fewer than 10 contacts. In other words, they've checked off the online Social/Professional networking box on their to-do list – they've joined the latest and greatest job search tool for the 21st Century – but they haven't done anything with it. They aren't investing the time and effort required to build up their Web of relationships or enrich them.

I call this situation the *Weak Link Syndrome*. It produces two harmful consequences.

- First, a lot of people in transition who have now joined professional networking sites believe they've strengthened their ability to find a new or better job, and they haven't. They think they're using a state-of-the-art tool to enhance their personal performance, and they aren't. They're wasting their time and talent fiddling with a technology – online professional networking – that isn't working for them.

- Second, the absence of so many job seekers networking effectively online has created a vacuum. And into that vacuum has flowed a crowd of individuals who are happy to misuse the system. Like my former connection on LinkedIn, they are clueless about the true nature of networking and feel entitled to use some malformed version of their own. And that misappropriation of the online networking experience diminishes it for everyone else.

So, what do I recommend? I think we have just two options. We can either devote the time and energy necessary to extend our online professional networks far beyond their current meager limits and then transform those contacts into genuine relationships or we should abandon the sites that are supposed to nurture them and turn our time and talent to more productive activities. As the old truism notes, *it's not worth doing something unless you're going to do it right.*

"Fairfillment": The Foundation for Fulfillment

At one point after the BP oil spill in the Gulf of Mexico, the CEO of the company released a video which revealed that the environmental damage was much greater than previously known. According to news reports, this information was in his possession for some time, but he chose not to provide it to the public. His act may not have been illegal, but it set a new low for ethics at work. And, it is the polar opposite of an emerging standard I call "fairfillment."

Today's workplace is seeing a growing number of men and women transform themselves into career activists. These individuals recognize that they (and everyone else) have been endowed with a talent – a capacity for excellence – and they are determined to express and experience that unique gift in the one-third of their life they spend on-the-job. A career activist works for their individual fulfillment, but believes the accomplishment of that end depends upon their first embracing fairness.

The dictionary defines the word *fair* as "being consistent with ethics." Hence, a career activist serves their own best interests by respecting the best interests of everyone else. They will not obey an illegal directive from their boss because harming the community or the planet prevents them from being fulfilled. They will not cut corners, shade the truth or hide dangerous situations because victimizing those around them diminishes both who they are and who they aspire to be.

Career activists, in effect, accept the responsibility for distinguishing between right and wrong actions in their work. American soldiers are expected to exercise such discretion in the heat of combat – when the calculus determines life or death – so career activists believe it is neither unrealistic nor asking too much to expect working men and women to do the same on-the-job. If the American people can demand that those who defend them do so in accordance with the Geneva Convention and the rules of war, then they should hold themselves to a similarly strict set of rules in their workplace behavior.

That commitment means more than simply adhering to the letter of the law. Certainly, career activists don't steal from their employers. But equally as important, they don't stoop to lying or cheating either. They are, for example, the human resource manager who refuses to backdate stock option grants for the executives in her company. They are the commissioned salesperson who will not sell an investment product he knows is defective. They are the engineer who refuses to approve construction work that is shoddy and dangerous even if it delays the project. And, they are the actuary who will not sign a financial statement they know to be untrue regardless of the pressure they get from their boss.

The Stand That Matters

Career activists do not set themselves up as the ethics police, but they do hold themselves to a high standard of personal conduct. They refuse to stoop to behavior that they know is wrong or to justify it as something they were "forced" to do by their superior. They strive to be the principled citizens of the workplace. Career activists will not work for organizations that condone, encourage or require illegal, unethical or inappropriate behavior. And if, by chance, they find themselves employed by one, they refuse to go along.

Career activists take such a stand knowing full well that it can have negative consequences. They may suffer the disapproval and even the public criticism of their supervisor. They might be ostracized by coworkers who are unwilling to hold themselves to a similar standard. They may see a decline in their performance evaluation and, therefore, lose a raise or promotion they would otherwise have earned. And, they might be fired because, ironically, they "don't live up to" the expectations of their employer.

There's no question that the impact of these consequences can be onerous and even damaging, especially in today's difficult economic climate. They can (temporarily) derail a person's progress in their career, undermine their financial security and impose a psychological or emotional burden on them and their family. The one thing these outcomes cannot do, however, is diminish their self-respect. Career activists are not perfect – they make the same mistakes and missteps as other people – but they always know that they have done so while reaching for the high bar of personal integrity. They may suffer setbacks along the way, but they never suffer a blow to their self-esteem.

A New MAD

Most Americans over the age of twenty-five remember the life-or-death struggle between the United States and the Soviet Union. Our security during those dangerous times depended on a strategic balance called "mutual assured destruction" or MAD. Today, we have another form of MAD, one that is most accurately defined as "mutual assured distraction." Instead of ensuring our wellbeing, however, it portends to undermine our job security and ultimately our career success.

The original MAD stood for a very simple, but powerful concept. Basically, it meant that both the U.S. and the Soviet Union had enough firepower in their arsenals to absorb a missile strike by the other and still wreck unacceptably high damages on the aggressor in a counter attack. Said another way, MAD ensured that any victory would be pyrrhic and thus not a logical course of action.

The new MAD has similar implications. To understand why that's so, however, we first have to recognize and accept a new fact of economic life. The Great Recession marked the start of a revolution in the American workplace. The competition in state, regional, national and global markets is now so intense and unforgiving, that America's employers have had to change their approach to how work gets done. They have infused massive levels of new technology into the workplace in order to upgrade the productivity of their operations. They have concluded that their survival is at risk if they don't deliver more and better quality output than their competitors, and they've decided that technology is the best way to do so.

If you have any doubt about the extent of this revolution, consider this. According to a new report by McKinsey & Company, U.S. employers are now so efficient in the way work is done that it will be at least 2020 before the country will create the same number of jobs the country had in 2007, before the recession began And, that's the most optimistic assumption.

This productivity revolution has also quietly and irrevocably changed the definition of a "qualified worker." It is now no longer enough to do a job. In order to be hired and then hold onto that job in this new environment, we have to excel at our work. We have to provide a contribution to our employer's productivity that is as great or greater than that which can be provided by technology. And, to put it bluntly, we can't perform at that level if we're constantly checking the latest updates we've received on LinkedIn, Twitter and Facebook.

The Assured Distraction of Social Media

Some claim that checking into social media sites on-the-job is a benign activity. Typically, they assert that it's no different than regularly checking one's email. It's something we can do without interrupting our concentration or diminishing our output. After all, we live in an era that celebrates multitasking as a way to get more done in the same amount of time.

But, here's the rub: the effectiveness of multitasking is an urban legend. Research confirms that whether you're 22 or 62, trying to do two things at once ensures that neither will be done well. By definition, one task interrupts the other, and such interruptions have a profoundly negative effect on productivity.

In one study reported in *Harvard Business Review*, for example, it took workers an average of 25 minutes to return to full effectiveness after an interruption. In another study commissioned by Hewlett Packard, researchers determined that the IQ scores of knowledge workers actually fell 10 points when they were regularly interrupted.

What's mutual about this distraction? Both parties – the sender and the receiver of social media communications – are harmed by the activity. Each interrupts their work performance, and each suffers potentially fatal damage to their productivity by doing so.

Checking social media on-the-job is, therefore, a form of "mutual assured distraction." And, distraction has consequences. We may have been able to get away with such behavior in the past. In today's hyper-demanding business environment, however, it is, to borrow a phrase, a formula for assured destruction … or what is best described as mad behavior.

Putting Innocence Aside

Recent news reports reveal that publishers have begun to slash the number of new children's picture books they are releasing each year. While that move will undoubtedly change the nature of early childhood for kids, it also signals a significant shift in the perspective of their parents. Adults are squeezing the innocence out of youth and in the process setting their own innocence aside. And, that development – more even than the stuttering job market – is cutting back on the potential in their future.

Parents, it seems, now want their youngsters to graduate to text as quickly as possible, so they can get on with the business of preparing for life in our modern economy. Mom and Dad are buying fewer of the books that tell their stories with colored images and visual portraits because they believe that the world doesn't work that way. And, I guess, in some respects that's true, but what have those kids lost in the process?

Unlike with passive pastimes – watching television, for example, or videos on YouTube – it takes creative energy to imagine a story told only or mostly in pictures. When a child "reads" *The Cat in the Hat* or *Good Night Moon*, they have to use their imagination to fill in what the words don't say. They have to create and invent, and in exercising their minds that way, they learn that they have the capacity to dream big, to step beyond the limitations of even their small bodies. And it's that innocence – that simple belief in their own magic – which is the foundation for what they can (and, hopefully, will) achieve as adults.

How Can Childhood Innocence Help Adults?

We live in an age that values reality. We force ourselves to acknowledge limited options. We push ourselves to make hard choices. And, of course, we fixate endless on the tyranny of the bottom line.

Not the stuff of fairy tales, to be sure. And yet, this is a nation built on innocence. It's that wondrous acceptance of our own magic which enables us to believe we will, in our lifetime, break down color, gender and other barriers that have existed for centuries. To believe we can find a way to free ourselves from the shackles of gravity and put a man on the moon in a single decade. To believe we have and will continue to triumph over closed and controlled states and offer the rest of the world, the most open, most welcoming, most prosperous and most generous nation on earth.

So, taking picture books away from kids may hurt them, but it hurts us parents as well. In the present, it reflects a decline in our own innocence, and in the future, it robs new adults of theirs. That loss can't be measured in dollars and cents. Economists can't calculate its opportunity cost, and chief financial officers can't tally up its impact on profits. But, every American knows the heavy toll we pay in dismissing our innocence. They sense it as the loss of the American Dream.

But innocence lost can also be found. We can reclaim what has been taken from us. We tell our kids stories of dragons and witches, not to have them dwell on what's frightening, but to imagine what can be overcome. The same is true with what afflicts us today in our adult kingdom.

The terrible recession, the stuttering recovery, the misery of a seemingly endless job search, the corruption of the universe's masters, all of that, is a fearful tale. It is one, however, in which we can write the ending. We can decide we are vanquished and doomed to despair, and we will be. Or, we can imagine ourselves rising to the challenge. That won't make the dragons any smaller, but it will make our resolve, our courage, and our possibility that much greater. If we picture ourselves as dragon slayers, we may be battered and bruised in the contest, but ultimately we will prevail.

That's the magic and the reality of innocence.

Taking the Me Out of Mediocrity

Mediocrity is understandably a touchy subject. Nobody thinks they are a middling performer. In fact, according to surveys, most of us believe we do a pretty good job at work. And, that may be true. The real issue, therefore, isn't whether we're doing a good job, but whether our good job is good enough to compete in the global marketplace.

The evidence would suggest that it's not. We've seen entire industries collapse and countless jobs move offshore. Cheap labor is partially responsible, to be sure, but so too is the caliber of our work. The good job we're doing is now less competitive than it once was. Others are matching what we do on-the-job, and they're delivering that output at a lower wage.

There are, of course, all kinds of reasons why this is happening. All too frequently, for example, our employers don't make it easy to excel on-the-job. They hire supervisors with the leadership skills of a brick. And, they introduce processes only a contortionist could love.

Those handicaps are real, but they don't change the essential nature of our challenge. We are in an economic battle that is more serious than any other we have ever faced. We're fighting to save our standard of living, and every other country on the planet (including those that are our allies) is waging the same war. They want to replace the American Dream with the Chinese Dream, the Indian Dream, the Brazilian Dream and the German Dream.

So, the question we have to ask ourselves is this: *Does our good job represent the absolute best job we can do?*

Generally speaking, most of us would probably answer that question in the affirmative. Sure, we all know those who haven't lived up to the standard. There are slackers in the workforce and, truth be told, all of us have probably cut a corner or two on occasion. By and large, however, most Americans have gone and continue to go to work each day and strive to do everything that's asked of them.

And that's what has changed. We now have to do more.

Putting Me Someplace Other Than in Mediocrity

We Americans have always done whatever it took to compete and win in the global economy. As a nation and as individuals, we set the bar that everyone else tried to reach. We established the definition of superior performance and delivered it on-the-job. Consciously or otherwise, we realized that working at such a level was the only way we could preserve and protect our standard of living, and we were determined to do so.

Meanwhile, the rest of the world watched and learned. They have taught themselves to imitate our standard. Not to flatter us, but to become our equals on-the-job. Our good job has become theirs, as well. And, in a highly competitive global marketplace, that equality of performance changes everything. It means that what was once superior is now simply mediocre. Everyone is doing it.

So, what can we do? Well, if everyone else around the world is now working up to our old standard, we will have to adopt a new one in order to prevail. In some cases, that may mean working harder than we have ever worked before. In others, it may involve injecting more creativity and innovation into what we do on-the-job and how we do it. But, in every instance and for every person, it will require that we commit ourselves to a new benchmark of excellence. We must take the Me out of mediocrity and put it into supreMe.

Now, some will say that such a notion is hyperbolic, that this radical redefinition of excellence simply isn't needed. But, it's hard to see how they can be right. A majority of Americans are now worried about the future (and even the present) of the American Dream. And, if we truly believe in that dream, shouldn't we be willing to make any effort, accept any sacrifice, endure any hardship to save it?

Yes, it will try men's and women's souls to face up to this challenge. Undoubtedly, it will demand more from us than we are accustomed to or even comfortable giving at work. But, the simple truth is that we must. The American Dream is what makes our nation exceptional. Each of us, therefore, has a stake in defining the standard for our era – what constitutes supreMe – and now is the moment we must do so.

The iPhone Proposition

Apple's iPhone has captured the popular imagination. Even among those who own a competitor, it has come to symbolize sleek styling, innovative features and ever more useful capabilities. That perception and the reality it celebrates are a perfect model for those of us who are seeking to advance their position with their current employer or searching for a better opportunity with another one.

Steve Jobs recognized that standing still is the single best way to fail in today's economy. Apple's competitors are always raising the bar in terms of design and performance, so it must too. Similarly, consumers are forever raising their expectations about what they want and need from a cell phone so Apple must oblige. In effect, those two inexorable forces mean that the only way Apple can survive and prosper is by working continuously at getting better.

The same dynamic also now impacts all of us in the workforce. Our competitors in the U.S. and abroad – those who want our job or the job we want – are upping their game and improving their ability to contribute to an employer's success. At the same time, employers now expect higher performance and harder work from both their current employees and those applying for their open positions. As a result, the only way we can survive and prosper in today's economy is by adopting the iPhone Proposition: we must work continuously to stay ahead of both our competitor's capabilities and our employers' expectations.

Sleek Styling, Innovative Features & Ever More Useful Capabilities

To replicate Apple's success and capture the imagination of employers – to set ourselves apart as a particularly valuable employee or candidate – we have to accomplish three tasks:

- We have to determine what skills and knowledge our current employer or prospective ones most want to see us provide;

- We have to acquire those skills and that knowledge even as we work at the job we have or look for a something better; and

- We have to make sure that the full set of our skills and knowledge is known to our current employer and those that could employ us in the future.

Let's look at each of these tasks in a bit more detail.

Task 1: Determining the skills and knowledge that employers want.

Unfortunately, most employers only advertise a portion of the skills and knowledge they would like to see in their candidates and employees. For the former, they describe them in job postings, and for the latter, they detail them in position descriptions. In today's highly competitive global marketplace, however, those stated qualifications aren't even the minimum necessary to be judged "fully qualified." What's often unstated but just as important are such ancillary skills as the ability to speak a second language, use the latest hardware or software in a particular field, or manage a diverse and dispersed team in the accomplishment of a key objective on time and within budget.

How can you determine what ancillary skills and knowledge are most important? Talk to managers who hire for the kind of position you seek, but don't ask them about the job; ask them about the characteristics they'd like to see in their perfect candidate. Focus on figuring out what kind of person they want to hire, not what requirements and responsibilities they've listed for the kind of job you want.

Task 2: Acquiring the skills and knowledge that employers want.

Fortunately, every ancillary skill and all of the latest knowledge are taught somewhere and increasingly, on a convenient schedule. Many traditional providers – academic institutions and commercial training vendors – now offer courses that are run before and after the normal business day. In addition, a wide variety of instruction is available on the Web and thus accessible 24/7 and from home or even on the road when traveling for business. The key to success with this task, however, is our mindset. It's not one and we're done. Acquiring skills and knowledge has become a permanent feature of our careers so we are never finished. Each of us, in effect, is a work-in-progress.

How do you justify making room for this new demand on your time when you probably already have a very overcrowded schedule? Look it as an investment in your future. Continuous self-improvement won't provide job security, but it will give you career security – the ability always to be employed and always by an employer of your choice.

Task 3: Making sure the full set of our skills and knowledge is known to employers.

Many of us fall into two traps when it comes to promoting our self-improvement efforts. First, we believe we should keep these activities to ourselves until they're complete. And second, we see such self-promotion as something that's unsavory or at least impolite.

Employers, however, are seeking personal attributes as well as skills in their employees and candidates. Informing them of on-going developmental efforts, therefore, is advantageous because it demonstrates two characteristics they value highly: initiative and self-reliance. Further, self-promotion isn't off-putting if it's done in a professional manner. The key is to focus on describing the potential value of the new skills and knowledge to the organization rather than on celebrating the sacrifice that's been made or the personal credential that's been earned.

How do you accomplish such professional self-promotion? If you're employed, it means taking the initiative during performance reviews and other meetings you schedule to keep your boss informed about your progress. And, if you're in transition, it means highlighting your on-going developmental effort on your resume.

The fact that you haven't finished isn't important. Whether you're an employee or an employment candidate, your goal is to establish yourself as a work-in-progress. That image will differentiate you from everyone else in the workforce who portrays themselves as done. Like the iPhone, it will say you are already good and always getting better. There's no better brand in the workplace.

The Metatarsal of Career Success

Scientists were thrilled to announce the other day that they had found a metatarsal bone in a skeleton that was millions of years old, proving that our earliest ancestors had been able to walk erect. While this bone in our foot was important to our early evolution, however, we need a very different kind of support to stand tall in the 21st Century workplace. We have to have just as much strength at the other end of our bodies – in our minds.

Our oldest known relative is Lucy, whose skeleton is believed to be 3.2 million years old. The fourth metatarsal was discovered in another skeleton believed to be contemporaneous with Lucy. It is a key bone in the human foot because it permits us to walk upright, and paleoanthropologists believe it was that unique posture which enabled our species to rise to the top of the evolutionary heap.

Standing erect gave Lucy and friends the mobility and breadth of vision to overcome the stronger creatures and challenges of nature they faced. Today, we need an equal degree of mobility and breadth of vision, but they will not be derived from our posture, but rather from our brains. We can't outrun or outmaneuver the market competitors that now endanger us, but we can outsmart them. And we must, because it is the quality of our thinking which will determine our survival and level of prosperity. It is the metatarsal of career success in the modern workplace.

Building a Strong Brain Every Day

It doesn't matter whether you're a rocket scientist or operating a robot on an assembly line, whether you're a sales clerk or a senior executive, the caliber of your job performance depends almost entirely on the intelligence and innovation you bring to work. By most estimates, however, we use only ten to twenty percent of our brains. In effect, we do our jobs with a good part of our intellectual ability tied behind our backs.

That may have been good enough in an industrial workplace, but it's a formula for extinction in a knowledge based economy. Most people already know that. They listen to the news; they see the government reports. But, they don't do anything that would untie their intelligence. Instead of upgrading their skills and knowledge, they continue to search for the fast disappearing kind of job that requires the use of a tiny fraction of their brain.

Why?

Because our culture has convinced them that only a very small percentage of people are "thinkers" and the rest of us are not. It's a widely held view that is an artifact of a school system that tracks kids by their academic performance and not their capacity for excellence. And, that's a mistake. Because every person is born with the inherent ability to apply their intellect and creativity to the accomplishment of tasks they find rewarding. That capacity is an attribute of our species. It is as much a part of who we are as a bone in our foot.

While we all know how to take care of our bones, however, many of us seem never to have learned how to take care of our minds. We know we have to nurture our bones so they'll grow and strengthen, yet we often act as if we can stop developing our brain just because we have an academic degree of some sort or have attained a certain level of seniority. And, that's simply not true. We live in a world of constant change, and that change requires that we adapt by continuously learning new concepts and capabilities. Moreover, all of us – whether we got good grades in school or not – have much more of our brains to tap into and bring to work.

We humans have come a long way since Lucy walked the grasslands of Africa. We were able to grow beyond that humble beginning because we refused to stand still. Physically to be sure, but with our minds, as well. Each of our ancestors saw themselves as a work-in-progress and so should we.

Things We Wish We Had Known

Cataclysmic events often alter our perceptions of the world around us. That was true during the Great Depression, and it will be true as we emerge from this Great Recession, as well. Some of these new views are opinions about what happened and why, but others are actually lessons that we've learned about how best to survive and prosper. They're the things we wish we had known before the event occurred because that knowledge would have undoubtedly enabled us to fare better than we did.

I think the sharing of this wisdom is good for us – it's cathartic to acknowledge that we've earned an advanced degree in the school of hard knocks – but it's even more helpful for our kids and grandkids. In a very real sense, we are giving them a gift, a roadmap for the future that may help them avoid the dead-ends and dangerous potholes they are sure to encounter.

Each of us has our own view of the lessons we should pass along. For me, the following four insights are among the most important. They are realizations everyone must have in order to chart a successful and fulfilling career in the 21st Century world of work.

Seeking job security makes you vulnerable.

In today's turbulent economy, employers have no idea what will happen tomorrow or the day after. They may promise you job security, but they can't deliver it. So, counting on it is likely to put you out for the count. A far better objective is career security – the ability to stay employed in a job of your choosing regardless of the condition of any single employer or the economy as a whole.

Unlike job security, career security is a state you create for yourself. You don't have to rely on the good will of some employer. You anticipate the changes in your career – the timing of a move from one boss or organization to another, the refocusing or reskilling that's necessary to accommodate shifts in your industry or profession – and then you plan and execute those changes so they benefit you.

Recognition is something you give yourself.

Most managers and supervisors mean well, but if you wait for them to recognize your accomplishments at work, you're likely to be disappointed. Some have the social skills of a brick and others are too worried about their own security to take care of yours.

That's why it's important for you to keep track of your own "career victories." Sure, it takes a little effort to maintain a contemporaneous record of what you've done and how well you've done it, but that account will give you more satisfaction than most managers ever will. Don't just write it out and forget about it, however; also review it regularly. Take the time to remember what you've done and pat yourself on the back when you deserve it or give yourself a little counseling if you've let yourself down.

Working tirelessly is a sure way to get tired.

Sadly, many people in today's world of work find themselves wired up with no place to go. They've learned the hard way that staying continuously in contact with the office doesn't protect you. It exhausts you. We're all worried about the flu or some new disease becoming a pandemic, but workaholism already is. If you have any doubt about that, look left and right the next time you're lying on the beach. Every other person will be glued to their Blackberry or iPhone checking their email from the office.

The impact of such behavior on both individual performance and well-being is already acute and likely to get worse. In a knowledge-based economy, your worth is measured not by your connectivity, but by your contribution. And, your contribution suffers when you don't give your mind and body a chance to rest.

Taking care of your career is the best way to take care of you.

The conventional approach to career self-management has been to get an annual checkup and leave it at that. Historically, we paid attention to our career just once each year – during our performance appraisal and salary review. That approach was dangerous then; today, it's a sure-fire way to induce career cardiac arrest or what most of us call unemployment.

The only safe course in a workplace as turbulent as the one we now have is to develop career fitness the same way you develop physical fitness. You have to commit yourself to building up the strength, endurance and reach of your career every single day. Yes, that's a lot of work, but it's also a smart investment. You spend one-third or more of your day in your profession, craft or trade, and you deserve an experience during that time that is every bit as good as the rest of your life.

We have acquired many insights from our experience over the past two years, but these four maxims are the key lessons we have learned. They are the things we wish we had known, but they can also be the lessons we use to shape our future.

About the Author

Peter Weddle has been the CEO of three HR consulting companies, a Partner in the Hay Group and the recipient of a Federal award for leadership-related research. Described by *The Washington Post* as "... a man filled with ingenious ideas," he has authored or edited over two dozen books and been a columnist for *The Wall Street Journal, National Business Employment Weekly* and CNN.com.

Weddle is now the CEO of WEDDLE's Research & Publications, a company which specializes in employment and workforce issues. WEDDLE's Guides to Internet employment sites are the gold standard of their genre, leading the American Staffing Association to call Weddle the "Zagat of the online employment industry." He also currently serves as the CEO of the International Association of Employment Web Sites, the trade organization for the global online employment services industry.

His most recent books, *The Career Activist Republic* and *Work Strong: Your Personal Career Fitness System*, offer a frank yet positive assessment of the challenges and opportunities available to working men and women in 21st Century America. His forthcoming novel, *A Multitude of Hope: A Novel about Rediscovering the American Dream*, is due out in early 2012.

Weddle is a graduate of the United States Military Academy at West Point. He has attended Oxford University and holds advanced degrees from Middlebury College and Harvard University.